How to Adjust and Keep Your Job

Dixie Lee Wright

jist
Publishing

Job Survival

How to Adjust and Keep Your Job

© 2000 by Dixie Lee Wright

Published by JIST Works, an imprint of JIST Publishing, Inc.
8902 Otis Avenue
Indianapolis, IN 46216-1033

Phone: 1-800-648-JIST   Fax: 1-800-JIST-FAX   E-Mail: info@jist.com

Visit JIST's Web Site at http://www.jist.com. Get additional information on JIST, free job search information and book chapters, and ordering information on our many products.

Other books by Dixie Lee Wright:
Know-How Is the Key Activity Book
Know-How Is the Key Instructional Manual

Development Editor: Susan Pines
Cover and Interior: Aleata Howard
Proofreader: Becca York

A Note to Instructors

The *Job Survival Instructor's Guide* (ISBN 1-56370-695-4) is available separately from JIST. The instructor's guide provides suggestions for in-class use of this workbook, plus additional information and activities. Quantity discounts are available for JIST books. Call 1-800-648-JIST for a free catalog and more information.

Printed in the United States of America

05 04 03 02 01   9 8 7 6 5 4 3 2

ISBN 1-56370-639-3

About This Book

This workbook will help you adjust and survive on your job. It is for anyone who has been out of the workplace for various reasons, has had trouble keeping a job, or has a situation that may affect job survival.

This workbook covers 11 key issues that are important to your job survival:

1. Change in the workplace
2. The importance of prioritizing
3. The effect of your attitude
4. Why you should use your best skills
5. How to set goals
6. Problem solving
7. The role of your good and bad habits
8. The magic of good manners
9. Why you should know your number 1 job responsibility
10. Why it is risky to break rules at work
11. How to deal with stress

Many of these issues involve your personal life, because this often overlaps with your work life. If you can deal with these issues in your personal life, your chances for job survival are much better.

To help you learn about these issues, two graphics appear throughout the workbook. Here is what they look like and what they mean:

Example

Real-life examples and stories are marked with this "Example" graphic. The examples help you understand the points being made.

Stop and Think

Worksheets, checklists, and questions are all marked by the "Stop and Think" graphic. When you see the lightbulb, take a few minutes to think about what you have just read. Answer the questions in the best way you can.

I hope this workbook helps you adjust to the workplace and survive on the job.

GOOD LUCK on YOUR JOB!

CONTENTS

PREFACE

This workbook is about you, your job, and your ability to stay on your job by *your* choice.

This is a working world. *By choice* are two very desirable words in the working world. Choice in one's working life is the ideal of every working person. The only way you can have freedom of choice is to be able to survive in this work world and move with it.

As a job retention specialist and coach, when I leave the work site after working with an employee, I always have a concern. My concern is not if the employee can do the job. It is, Can the employee keep the job? This is a concern regardless of the job level.

This workbook is for those who have been out of the workplace for various reasons or are having trouble keeping a job. I refer to these people as individuals with *different job needs than the average worker.*

The work world is constantly changing, and there is stuff you need to know about the workplace. This information is needed if you are to survive. This information is needed if you are to have a choice in retention and advancement.

People with different job needs do not lose their jobs because they cannot do their jobs. They lose their jobs because they cannot adjust to the working environment.

Why can't they adjust? They are not prepared for today's workplace. Failure to adjust to the workplace is costing jobs. Many people with different job needs cannot survive on the job long enough to prove their worth.

When is there a possibility of being fired or quitting? The answer: the moment you start the job.

It is like running a race. You either get stronger, learn how to cope, overcome problems, overcome discomfort, and meet the demands of training to go for the win. Or, you give up because you do not see the win for yourself.

If you want to survive, there is STUFF YOU NEED TO KNOW.

Acknowledgment
My special thanks to my husband, Lendon, for his encouragement and his endless hours on the computer in putting this book together. I could not have done it without him.

CHAPTER 1

This chapter will help you

- See that the workplace is always changing—and that you must adjust.

- Deal with your personal needs and barriers.

- Prepare for labeling and complaints.

- Decide what type of worker you want to be.

YOUR WAKE-UP CALL

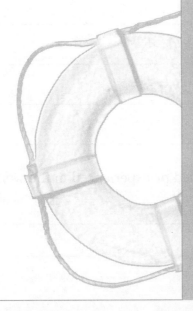

This is your SURVIVAL WAKE-UP CALL.

The work world is changing rapidly.

You need to see the work site as it is, not as you would like it to be.

You must adjust to the work site. The work site will not adjust to you.

To survive a job in the real world, here is REAL STUFF YOU NEED TO KNOW.

Wake Up: Be Aware of the Changing Workplace

The world and the workplace are always changing. Changes are good, but changes can catch you by surprise if you are not awake.

EXAMPLE

Look at the following list. Use it as a reminder of changes in the last 25 years.

Dress code	Holiday pay	Electronics
Television	Smoking policy	Job restrictions
Recreational facilities	High pressure	Job-related laws
Credit cards	Pension plan	Benefits
Transportation	Health	Child-care provisions
Exercise	Working hours	Eating habits
Sick leave	Technology	Restaurants
Sports	Job security	Marriage
		Movies

STOP AND THINK

1. Think back to when you were in middle school or junior high school. What changes have occurred since then? _____

_____

_____

_____

2. List any changes that you have observed or experienced in the workplace:

_____

_____

_____

The workplace is changing very fast. Global competition, population growth, and technology are some factors that make everything move so quickly. You must be ready to change too.

Wake up and SEE THE CHANGES.

The Effects of These Changes

The changing world has affected the work world in many ways. The work site structure has changed. Workers, including management, come and go. Technology is everywhere. When the work world changes, it affects the daily lives of people.

STOP AND THINK

Review the changes you listed in the two questions on pages 2 and 3. Then answer the questions here.

1. Have these changes affected your overall daily life? Yes ___   No ___

   Please explain: _____

   _____

   _____

2. Were they good changes or bad changes? Please explain:_____

   _____

(continues)

(continued)

3. Have these changes affected your work life? Yes ___ No ___

Please explain: _____

_____

_____

4. Have these changes affected members of your family? Yes ___ No ___

Please explain: _____

_____

_____

5. Have these changes affected your neighborhood? Yes ___ No ___

Please explain: _____

_____

_____

When the world changes, the workplace changes. When the workplace changes, your work site changes.

EXAMPLE

Changes create unexpected issues. In the past, a family member could pick up a child who got sick at school. The relative could keep the child until you got off work. No more. Almost every family member works.

Another unexpected issue is bad traffic. Almost everyone drives. Many families have two cars. Traffic has changed in your neighborhood and in your city.

You need to be prepared to deal with unexpected issues every day. You need to be on the job and do your job every day. If not dealt with, unexpected issues can cost you your job.

Adjust to the Multicultural Workplace

One big change is the multicultural work site. What is a multicultural work site? It is a work site made up of many different people. These people are of many races, social behaviors, ethnic beliefs, religious beliefs, and backgrounds.

STOP AND THINK

1. Has the multicultural work site affected you? Yes ___ No ___

2. Has it affected you personally, a member of your family, or a friend? Yes ___ No ___

3. Have you observed multicultural work sites in which you were not satisfied with the service? Yes ___ No ___

4. Write a short statement about a good experience you have had personally at a multicultural work site: _____

   _____

   How did the experience make you feel? _____

   _____

5. Write a short statement about a bad experience you had personally with a multicultural work site: _____

   _____

   How did the experience make you feel? _____

   _____

You work in a multicultural work site. You need to get along with people from different cultures and backgrounds. This requires adjusting and readjusting, because it will always be changing.

You have to find a way to
ADJUST TO THESE CHANGES.

Wake Up: Identify Your Personal Needs to Keeping a Job

In today's workplace, many different people have many different needs. A different personal need is something you know or suspect is a barrier to keeping your job. Think about a different need or barrier that may stop you from keeping a job.

Being ready to deal with your needs is part of your wake-up call. You have to find a way to deal with your personal needs to keep your job.

STOP AND THINK

Look over the following list. It contains ordinary needs and issues that most persons have to deal with before getting or keeping a job.

Your needs may be the same as everyone else who takes a job (like needing a dependable way to get to work). Your needs may be entirely different than most people who take a job (like having problems with a background check).

1. Circle anything that is a barrier for you in getting or keeping a job:

Transportation	Following directions	Regulated hours
Reading skills	Background check	Salary requirement
Location	Physical requirements	Sitting
Child care	Mental requirements	Standing
Listening	Appropriate clothing	Technology knowledge

Math skill	A.M. or P.M. shift	Mobility
Lifting requirements	Balance	Dexterity
Spelling skills	Eyesight	On-the-job training
Communication skills	Hearing	

2. List three needs you have that you consider to be entirely different than most persons' needs in keeping a job:

_____

_____

_____

You know that you have different needs that could be a barrier. Consider these issues carefully.

Think More About Your Different Needs

You have identified what you think are your different needs to consider when trying to survive on the job. It is important for you to stop and think about your different needs.

STOP AND THINK

1. Look at the three needs you have listed above. List them again:

_____

_____

_____

(continues)

(continued)

2. Why do you think these needs are different than those of most people? _____

_____

_____

3. When did you discover these needs? _____

_____

_____

4. How might these needs affect your job survival? _____

_____

_____

5. How are you going to make up for these different needs? _____

_____

_____

If you think you can overcome these issues if given the chance, then deal with them. If you think it will be difficult to overcome these issues, then reconsider the job. Look for work where these needs will not get in the way of your job survival.

JOB SURVIVAL is very important.

If you know that you have a different need, you will have to deal with this different need sooner or later. You must talk about this issue with your employer. It is necessary for keeping the job.

Are You Able to Admit Your Different Needs?

EXAMPLE

Many people with a different need—whether it is lack of education, a record, a disability, a language barrier, or lack of experience—will deny that they have a different need. They convince themselves that no one will know and it will be OK. It probably will *not* be OK. It probably will interfere with your job survival.

STOP AND THINK

1. Do you have a different need? Yes ___ No ___

   If yes, are you always able to admit it? Yes ___ No ___

2. Have you ever been unable to do a job? Yes ___ No ___

   If yes, were you able to admit it? Yes ___ No ___

3. Have you ever not understood what to do on the job? Yes ___ No ___

   If yes, were you able to admit it? Yes ___ No ___

4. Explain your answers for the three questions above: _____

   _____

   _____

   _____

Do not start or continue a job in denial. Take ownership of your different needs. Confront them. Make a decision about how you can or cannot survive on the job. Talk to someone you trust or your employer. Do not try to fool yourself or your employer. It will hurt your job survival.

Wake Up: Recognize Labeling in the Workplace

Labeling happens in the workplace. Labeling is when people make statements about other people. Labeling may be happening to you. This is another part of your wake-up call.

Do you recognize labeling in the workplace? Do you think statements made about you, or by you, are just idle comments? What is the message? Why are coworkers making these comments? What is the point of the statement?

Have you ever LABELED SOMEONE?

STOP AND THINK

1. Have you ever labeled someone? Yes ___ No ___

2. Have you ever been labeled? Yes ___ No ___

3. Look at the following table. It shows statements people make about other people. These statements are heard every day in the workplace.

   In the margin, check statements or similar statements you have made about a friend, neighbor, family member, or coworker. Then follow the next directions in questions 4 and 5.

Statement	What Is the Label?
I don't believe her.	
He is not smart enough to do that.	
She lies all the time.	

Statement	What Is the Label?
You can't believe a word he says.	
She has a big problem.	
He is as slow as can be.	
He is too lazy to work.	
She is a con.	
It is never her fault.	
He always blames someone else for his failures.	
She hasn't got the sense she was born with.	
She procrastinates all the time.	
You just can't trust him.	
I am tired of paying taxes so they can stay home.	
They should go back where they came from.	
He was too dumb to get through school.	
They would rather have babies than work.	
She is a psycho.	
He never does his part.	

(continues)

(continued)

> 4. Go back and put an "L" by any statement or similar statement you have heard coworkers use in describing a friend, neighbor, family member, or other coworker.
>
> 5. Look again at your list. What are you or your coworkers really saying? Write your answers in the column "What Is the Label?"

Recognizing the indirect label is very important in the workplace. Beware of idle comments. You must realize that when coworkers drop casual remarks about another coworker, it sends a labeling message. Be prepared for casual remarks about you.

Prepare for Labeling in the Workplace

Idle comments or casual statements repeated several times about someone will become a label. Once you have a label (good or bad) in the workplace, it will stick.

STOP AND THINK

Look at your list on pages 10 and 11. If you have checked more than one statement, you need to look inside yourself. Why would you consider using these statements about another person?

1. List three of the statements and explain under what circumstances you would use them.

Statement 1: _____

_____

_____

Statement 2: _____

_____

_____

Statement 3: _____

_____

_____

2. Now count the "L"s you have written. ____ What have you discovered? _____

_____

_____

This is called LABELING.

Labeling can destroy a worker on the work site. Do not repeat labels that have been put on coworkers. It can destroy them. You must get prepared to overcome any labels that may be put on you.

If you are labeled, confront the persons who are labeling you. Be pleasant but straightforward. You need to know why these persons feel the need to label you.

If handled right, most people will stop using the label. If this does not work, mention it to your supervisor. Do not do this in anger. Try not to give names.

You Must Deal with Complaints About You

Why should you care if coworkers label you or complain about you? You have to care about what coworkers say about you. Too many complaints by coworkers can get you fired. Whether it is fair or not, you must deal with it.

STOP AND THINK

List as many reasons as you can think of why coworker complaints might affect your work:

(continues)

(continued)

1. _____	6. _____
2. _____	7. _____
3. _____	8. _____
4. _____	9. _____
5. _____	10. _____

Do not take coworkers' complaints lightly. Remember, you are a part of a team. Too many complaints, and it destroys teamwork. Management will let you go. It affects the team, which affects the profits.

Select a member of your work team to talk with in confidence and away from the work site. Ask why you are drawing complaints. Show concern, not anger. Be willing to listen. Ask for suggestions on how to correct the complaints. If you are not comfortable approaching someone on your team, choose someone else at the work site to find out for you.

Understand Your Feelings About Coworkers

Chances are if you do not like certain coworkers, it is because strong feelings are involved. Chances are if you like certain coworkers, it is because strong feelings are involved. These strong feelings can affect your work and your team.

If you do not understand why you feel the way you do, then how can you understand the reactions of other persons? Wake up. Think about these feelings.

STOP AND THINK

1. On the facing page is a list of types of persons in the workplace. Select two types of persons you definitely would like to work with. Describe these two persons as if you were writing in your diary and only you will read it: _____

_____

_____

_____

_____

2. Now select two types of persons you definitely would not like to work with. Describe these two persons as if you were writing in your diary and only you will read it: _____

_____

_____

_____

Remember, this is labeling. BE CAREFUL.

Hyper	Cheat	Complainer	Courteous	Honest
Nasty	Fat	Dumb	Handsome	Good-looking
Rude	Lazy	Mean	Cheerful	Mannerly
Troublemaker	Crazy	Freak	Polite	Dependable
Thief	Jerk	Smart	Friendly	Truthful
Liar	Foreigner	Funny	Ethical	Good guy
Ugly	Jailbird	Sharp	Generous	Loud
Gossip	Weird	Helpful	Creative	Positive

Be the type of person you would like to work with. Definitely do not be the type of person you would *not* like to work with. If you would not like to work with this type of person, then nobody else will either.

Wake Up: What Type of Worker Are You?

It is important to decide what type of worker you would like to be in the always-changing workplace. This is part of your wake-up call for job survival.

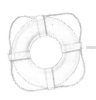

It is important that you observe other workers. You will see what you like and what you do not like. It will help you make your decision.

STOP AND THINK

1. Write a description of yourself as a worker in the workplace. Consider your strengths and weaknesses. Be honest about yourself. _____

   _____

   _____

   _____

2. Review your description. What did you discover about yourself? _____

   _____

   _____

3. Give your description to someone else to read, without revealing that it is you. Ask this person to write a short statement in your workbook about this person as a coworker: _____

   _____

   _____

4. What did you discover from someone else's view of the description? _____

   _____

   _____

If you like the type of coworker you have described, then make up your mind to be this type of worker.

You can be great stuff. YOU ARE AWAKE!

CHAPTER 2

This chapter will help you

- Learn different ways to prioritize.

- See how your values and principles affect your priorities.

- Consider other issues that affect prioritizing.

- Know that your priorities will change.

PRIORITIZING

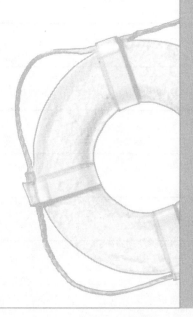

**This is your
SURVIVAL POWER.**

The practice of prioritizing can mean success or failure in most paths you will take.

Prioritizing forces you to focus on first things first.

This is REAL STUFF YOU NEED TO FOCUS ON.

The Importance of Prioritizing

Your challenge is to adjust to the workplace and to keep the job. This sounds simple, but it is not.

You have a greater chance of success if you know what your priorities are. Prioritizing means that you will start to put first things first.

A Way to Prioritize:
Take It Step by Step

To prioritize areas of your life, you need to start looking at and organizing the things you do. One simple way to prioritize is to make a list of tasks you need to do. Then put the tasks in order, from beginning to end.

 ## STOP AND THINK

Since this workbook is on job survival, let's look at a work-world issue. For example, you must take certain steps to job search successfully.

Look at the tasks in the left column. In the right column, list the tasks in the order you would do them. This is a form of prioritizing.

Tasks When Looking for a Job	Tasks in the Order You Would Do Them
Identify skills	1.
Identify interests	2.
Set goals	3.
Fill out applications	4.
Interview	5.
Write cover letters	6.
Write resume	7.

Tasks When Looking for a Job	Tasks in the Order You Would Do Them
Analyze attitude	8.
Overcome barriers	9.
Network	10.

Prioritizing will keep you focused on your goals. Prioritizing in its simplest form—sitting down and making a list—is the fastest way to organize yourself. This will work on the job and in your personal life.

If you want to be successful, PUT FIRST STEPS FIRST.

A Way to Prioritize: Compare Important Matters with Each Other

The only way you can truly prioritize is to compare important matters with each other. Then you will know what is most important to you and where you should focus your time, energy, and other resources.

STOP AND THINK

This is another exercise in prioritizing. With this method, you will be able to list items according to their importance to you.

I want you to compare every fruit to all other fruits to see which one you like the best. First you will compare a banana to all other fruits, then an apple to all other fruits, and so on:

Do you like banana better than apple?

Write banana or apple on line B under banana.

(continues)

(continued)

Do you like banana better than orange?

Write banana or orange on line C under banana.

Do you like banana better than grape?

Write banana or grape on line D under banana.

Do you like banana better than plum?

Write banana or plum on line E under banana.

Do you like banana better than peach?

Write banana or peach on line F under banana.

A. Banana   Banana

B. Apple   B. _____   Apple

C. Orange   C. _____   C. _____   Orange

D. Grape   D. _____   D. _____   D. _____   Grape

E. Plum   E. _____   E. _____   E. _____   E. _____   Plum

F. Peach   F. _____   F. _____   F. _____   F. _____   F. _____

Every line under banana should now have a fruit listed on it.

Now go to apple and compare it to fruits C through F. Write your answers under apple. Then go to orange and compare it to fruits D through F. Write your answers under orange. Continue through the entire fruit list. When you have finished, count how many times you have listed each fruit.

List each fruit below, going from the fruit you listed the most to the one you listed the least:

1. _____   4. _____

2. _____   5. _____

3. _____   6. _____

Now you know which fruits you like best.

Sometimes you will be surprised at what is really number one. You can try this approach with other issues in your work and life.

A Way to Prioritize: Identify Values and Principles

Your values and your principles will help you decide what is important. Knowing what is important to you will help you prioritize.

What you value may change in your lifetime. Principles rarely change. You must identify what you value and what you hold as principles.

- What is a value? A value is a thing that has worth, usefulness, or importance to the possessor.

- What is a principle? A principle is a standard or a quality considered worthwhile or desirable.

EXAMPLE

Your values today are very important. One reason you work is to pay for the things you value, such as your own place to live or new clothes. The number one reward for doing a job is money. Without the prospect of money, many changes will be forced in your life. The ability to protect and promote the things you value will motivate you to stay on the job. You will try harder.

Not all things you value can be bought. For example, you may value your free time and your friendships.

Your principles are very important. If you have to compromise a principle, then your job survival is in question. For example, if telling the truth is one of your principles, then you may choose to leave a company that is not truthful to employees.

You may be making the salary you need, but it is hard to compromise a strong principle over time. You will be unhappy and will probably not stay with the company.

STOP AND THINK

Look at the list below. Put a "V" in front of an item if you think it is something of value to people. Put a "P" in front of an item if you think it is a principle or if it goes against a principle.

____ Clothes		____ Steal
____ Money		____ Jewelry
____ Honesty		____ Do drugs
____ Housing		____ Car
____ Fight at work		____ Drink alcohol
____ Gossip		____ Punctuality
____ Food		____ Good sense of humor
____ Education		____ Break a promise
____ Good health		____ Privacy
____ Freedom		____ Break into someone's home

If a job does not support the things you value, you will not stay on the job. If a job goes against your principles, you will not stay on the job very long. So knowing your values and principles will give you survival power.

You may choose to sacrifice a value. But it is more difficult to sacrifice a principle. Your values and principles will help you set priorities and put first things first. Know your values and your principles.

Your Important Values Today

A reminder: Values may change in your lifetime. What you put worth on today may change as you grow older or by circumstances. You are looking at your values today.

Values are things that you feel have great worth and importance.

STOP AND THINK

List six values that are important to you:

1. _____   4. _____

2. _____   5. _____

3. _____   6. _____

Rank them according to their importance to you:

1. _____   4. _____

2. _____   5. _____

3. _____   6. _____

Many times what people think they value most are really lower on their lists. Prioritizing your values will give you a true picture.

Prioritize Your Values

Why is so much importance put on values? Values are usually the main reason most people work. You work to support what you think is important in your life.

STOP AND THINK

Prioritizing your values will help you see what is most important to you. Look at your values list above. List your values below:

A. _____   D. _____

B. _____   E. _____

C. _____   F. _____

(continues)

(continued)

Compare each value to your other values, just as you did with fruits:

Do you value A or B more?
Write answer on line B under value A.

Do you value A or C more?
Write answer on line C under value A.

Do you value A or D more?
Write answer on line D under value A.

Do you value A or E more?
Write answer on line E under value A.

Do you value A or F more?
Write answer on line F under value A.

Value A

B. _____ Value B

C. _____ C. _____ Value C

D. _____ D. _____ D. _____ Value D

E. _____ E. _____ E. _____ E. _____ Value E

F. _____ F. _____ F. _____ F. _____ F. _____

Now go to value B and compare it to values C through F. Write your answers under value B. Then go to value C and compare it to values D through F. Write your answers under value C. Continue through the entire list.

Count how many times you have listed each letter above. Then list the corresponding values, going from the value you listed the most to the one you listed the least:

1. _____   4. _____

2. _____   5. _____

3. _____   6. _____

These are the things YOU VALUE MOST. Any SURPRISES?

People are usually surprised at what their top values really are.

Remember, your values today are your values today. They can change. But today's values must take priority. You cannot ignore these values. They must be a part of taking and working a job or you will not survive.

EXAMPLE

If you value funky casual clothes, you will be uncomfortable and unhappy on a job with a strict, conservative dress code. This could interfere with your job duties. You will not think you fit with this group. You may feel out of place. The company may feel you are out of place. It could cost your job. The fit is very important. You may not have considered the importance of your dress before taking the job.

Other Issues to Consider When Prioritizing

When setting priorities, you need to consider other issues. These issues are discussed in the following sections.

Everyday Matters That May Interfere with Job Survival

Sometimes you take a job but do not think about the priorities in your daily life that will interfere with your job. Some things are so important that unless they are dealt with, you cannot succeed on the job.

EXAMPLE

Suppose that you do not own a car. You must rely on a bus for transportation. Working your life into bus schedules is a priority for you. You are bus savvy and never considered transportation a problem or a priority when taking the job.

However, your job requires you to work on Saturday, and the Saturday bus schedule is very tight. You did not consider that the bus schedule changes on Saturday. You cannot guarantee your employer that you will always be on time on Saturday. This is interfering with your job, because you must be on time to keep your job. This will interfere with your job survival.

STOP AND THINK

Check anything that may interfere with the job you have taken:

_____ Day care	_____ Working weekends
_____ Working alone	_____ Allergies
_____ Working with people	_____ Working holidays
_____ Transportation	_____ Reading ability
_____ Clothing	_____ Doctor appointments
_____ Outdoor work	_____ Math ability
_____ Indoor work	_____ Weight
_____ Sick children	_____ Health
_____ Working nights	_____ Spelling

____ Budget

____ Writing

____ Speaking

____ Speed

____ Phone skills

____ Computer skills

____ Location

____ Family members

If you do not take time to look at the common everyday things that are important to your job survival, you take a great risk. You must prioritize taking care of these issues as well.

JOB SURVIVAL is at RISK.

Your Personal Time

Everyone has personal priorities that must be met away from the work site on private time. Your private time is limited and very valuable. You must make room in your schedule for this private time if you are going to remain healthy in body and mind. It will make you a better person and a better employee.

Do not put off until tomorrow what you should have done yesterday.

Health

STOP AND THINK

What do you do for your health? List three things:

1. _____

2. _____

3. _____

Relaxation

STOP AND THINK

What do you do for relaxation? List three things:

1. _____

2. _____

3. _____

Education

STOP AND THINK

What do you do to continue your education? List three things:

1. _____

2. _____

3. _____

Spiritual

STOP AND THINK

What do you do to help your inner self? List three things:

1. _____

2. _____

3. _____

You must be able to balance your work life and your personal life. You must make time to take care of yourself. You cannot do a good job at work if you have not taken care of yourself. You will not survive the job.

Shared and Total Responsibilities

When you are working, it is difficult to imagine how you can fit one more thing into your day. It is important that you realize how many responsibilities in a day or week are yours totally and how many can be shared.

EXAMPLE

You may be a single parent with children who are not old enough to drive or grocery shop. But they may be old enough to help with cooking.

Sharing some responsibilities will give you more time for your priorities and help your job survival.

STOP AND THINK

What responsibilities do you have to do yourself? What responsibilities can be shared with a family member, friend, child-care provider, or someone else?

Totally Your Responsibility	Shared Responsibility

Many times you have been used to doing everything yourself. You do not realize that some responsibilities can be done by someone else. If you can share certain responsibilities with someone else, such as children, parents, spouses, friends, neighbors, sitters, and hired help, you can free up time in your week. You can make time for yourself and other priorities.

IT WILL MAKE YOUR WORKING LIFE BETTER and longer lasting.

How Your Life Affects Your Priorities

Events in your life change you and affect your priorities. It is important that you look at your past and realize changes that have sent you in different directions.

Were they good changes or bad changes for you? Reflection is good. It helps you prioritize what is important today.

EXAMPLE

Your parents divorced when you were 12 years old. You moved from apartment to apartment for a period of time. One of your top priorities might be to buy a big house and live in it forever. This would have a tremendous effect on your choice of jobs.

Priorities for you would be location, possibility of transferring, possibility of advancement, salary, company financials, and the demand for your type of work in this community. Your past will influence your priorities.

STOP AND THINK

Below is a lifeline starting at age 12. Mark an "X" anyplace on that lifeline that a significant change happened in your life. Your past may have influenced your priorities, especially in the area of work.

Your Lifeline

12 13 14 15 16 17 18 19 20 21 22 23 24 25 26 27 28
29 30 31 32 33 34 35 36 37 38 39 40 Other

Many people do not like change. Many people are afraid of change and will remain where they are even though it may not be good for them. This is especially true when it is job related. Many people welcome change. They view it as a challenge and will work harder to succeed. This is especially true if it is job related.

STOP AND THINK

Look at your lifeline and where you marked your "X"s indicating a change.

1. Did the changes have anything to do with a job, either yours or someone else's?
   Yes_____ No_____ Please explain: _____

   _____

2. Did the changes have anything to do with money? Yes_____ No_____ Please explain:

   _____

3. Did the changes have anything to do with priorities? Yes_____ No_____ Please

   explain: _____

   _____

Job-related issues cause many changes in life. More problems are created and resolved over job-related issues than any other single issue. This is a working world. The choice of job survival is a necessary thing for most people. Prioritizing will help to accomplish this.

Is Keeping Your Job a Priority?

If you have the determination to be a winner on the job, then priorities are absolutely necessary for success. You have also made the decision that you will stay on the job until you are a winner, regardless of how long it takes.

I have been told that experts estimate that it takes two to five years to master most jobs. It would take mastering the job to be a winner. Therefore, you must evaluate your life priorities very carefully, because they play a big part in your job survival.

HOW CAN YOU KNOW WHEN TO HOLD AND WHEN TO FOLD on a job?

Every so often, you need to evaluate where you are with your job. Do you need or want to hold on to it? Or is it time to consider folding and making a change? How can you know when to hold and when to fold on a job?

STOP AND THINK

Check anything that you need to take a hard look at:

_____ Is the work challenging?

_____ Is the work stressful?

_____ Do the boss and you tangle?

_____ Do you get along with most coworkers?

_____ Do you fit in?

_____ Are you in a dead-end job?

_____ Are you mediocre at your job?

_____ Are you making enough money?

_____ Do you have job security?

_____ Is there too much traveling to get to the job?

_____ Is the work site too crowded?

_____ Are you fast enough?

_____ Are you accurate enough?

_____ Are you happy with your job?

_____ Is your job just ok?

_____ Is your job supporting your values and principles?

_____ Can you get another job easily?

When you know your priorities, you are in a position to make job choices for yourself. Choice of jobs, choice of job retention, and choice of change are what everyone hopes to have in his or her working life. Know your priorities. They will help you survive on the job. They are your survival power.

CHAPTER 3

This chapter will help you

- Recognize your attitude in the workplace.

- See the effects of your attitude.

- Fix your attitude.

ATTITUDE

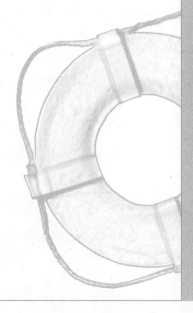

**This is your
SURVIVAL TOOL.**

Your attitude can determine what you achieve in the workplace.

Good or bad, if you keep doing what you are doing, you will keep getting what you are getting.

A good attitude will help you in the workplace. A bad attitude will hurt you.

This is TRUE STUFF YOU NEED TO KNOW.

What Is an Attitude?

An attitude is your feeling toward something. It can also be your manner or state of mind. Your attitude can be good or bad.

But it becomes automatic. No matter how you define attitude, it is always showing.

STOP AND THINK

Take time to identify the traits that people think of as attitudes. Check mark the attitudes that apply to you:

_____ Adaptable	_____ Easygoing
_____ Aggressive	_____ Explosive
_____ Angry	_____ Fair
_____ Blunt	_____ Flaky
_____ Bossy	_____ Good-natured
_____ Broad-minded	_____ Grumpy
_____ Bullheaded	_____ Hardheaded
_____ Calculating	_____ Honest
_____ Careful	_____ Impatient
_____ Careless	_____ Intense
_____ Compassionate	_____ Initiator
_____ Considerate	_____ Jittery
_____ Deceitful	_____ Jolly
_____ Daydreamer	_____ Kind
_____ Dependable	_____ Lazy
_____ Depressed	_____ Leader

____ Manic	____ Risk taker
____ Motivated	____ Skeptical
____ Nice	____ Show-off
____ Nutty	____ Stubborn
____ Open-minded	____ Sweet
____ Passive	____ Team player
____ Prompt	____ Two-faced
____ Pleasant	____ Reliable
____ Quick-tempered	____ Vocal
____ Quiet	____ Weak
____ Respectful	____ Well-rounded

The word *attitude* sends a strong meaning about someone. When someone says you have an attitude, everyone knows what it means. If the word itself is so strong, then it deserves special attention.

Make your attitude good. It is ALWAYS SHOWING.

The Effects of Attitude in the Workplace

At work, your attitude can be more important than your skills. Skills can be improved by training. If you have a good attitude, your boss and coworkers may help you improve your skills. But only you can improve your attitude.

Your attitude will affect your productivity. Your attitude will also affect the following:

- Coworkers
- Customers
- Schedules
- Accuracy
- Work quantity
- Work quality

All these things affect profits. A good attitude is your job survival tool.

STOP AND THINK

It is important that you become aware of good and bad attitudes in the workplace. You should also become aware of their effects.

The best way to see the effects of good and bad attitudes is to look at the effects of coworkers' attitudes.

1. List some bad attitudes in the workplace: _____

_____

_____

_____

2. List some effects of bad attitudes in the workplace: _____

_____

_____

_____

3. List some good attitudes in the workplace: _____

_____

_____

_____

4. List some effects of good attitudes in the workplace: _____

_____

_____

_____

Your attitude is your feeling toward some matter. Stay aware of good and bad attitudes. A good attitude can make a big difference on the work site.

Your attitude affects YOUR JOB SURVIVAL.

The Effects of Attitude on Coworkers

If you are doing your job, you may feel that your attitude is no one's business. This is risky. Your attitude affects your job, your coworkers, and people you service around you.

Your coworkers can "catch" your attitude. Your coworkers will not want to work with you. They may avoid you. They may complain about you. Your bad attitude will affect the work of those on your team.

EXAMPLE

No one wants to be around someone with a bad attitude. Do you like being around someone who is a complainer, negative, or lazy? Would you rather be around someone who is friendly, cooperative, or upbeat? A bad attitude means trouble on the work site.

STOP AND THINK

Do you think you have a good attitude most of the time in the workplace?
Yes ___ No ___

Do you think you have a bad attitude most of the time in the workplace?
Yes ___ No ___

Name six reasons why coworkers want to work with you:

1. _____

2. _____

3. _____

4. _____

5. _____

6. _____

Name six reasons why you want to work with coworkers who have good attitudes:

1. _____

2. _____

3. _____

4. _____

5. _____

6. _____

Name six reasons why coworkers do not want to work with you:

1. _____

2. _____

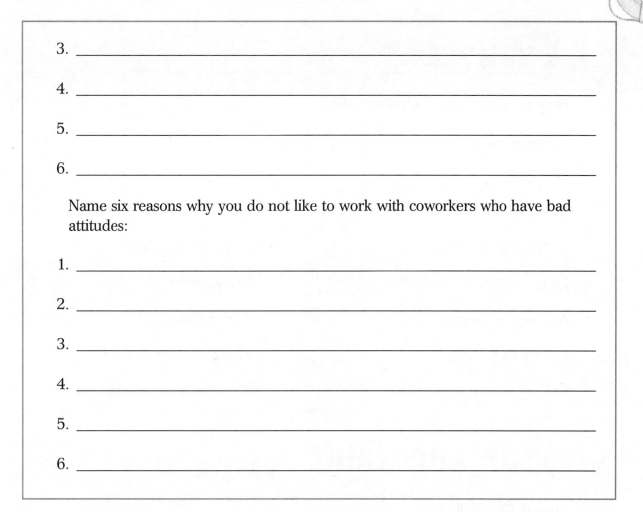

3. _____

4. _____

5. _____

6. _____

Name six reasons why you do not like to work with coworkers who have bad attitudes:

1. _____

2. _____

3. _____

4. _____

5. _____

6. _____

Attitudes are catching. Try to catch what you like about coworkers with good attitudes. Try *not* to catch what you dislike about coworkers with bad attitudes.

Your friends may accept a poor attitude. Your family may put up with a poor attitude. But your coworkers and employer cannot afford your poor attitude.

Make your attitude good. It is a survival tool.

Signs of a Bad Attitude in the Workplace

Be aware of signs that start to show a bad attitude in the workplace.

EXAMPLE

Here are some signs of a bad attitude:

Talking about the boss	Breaking rules
Gossiping	Making fun of coworkers
Clocking in late	Criticizing the work of others
Calling in sick often	Using bad language
Lying	Dirty clothes
Abusing the telephone	Back talking
Leaving early	Customer complaints
Refusing to help a coworker	Comments on your attitude

STOP AND THINK

Look at the list above.

1. Are you showing any of these signs in your workplace? Yes ___ No ___

   Explain the signs: _____

   _____

   _____

2. Are your coworkers showing any of these signs? Yes ___ No ___

   Explain the signs: _____

   _____

   _____

You have identified reasons why you do not want to work with certain coworkers. A bad attitude may not be the only reason. But it may be one big reason. It may also be a reason why someone does not want to work with you.

Remember, YOUR ATTITUDE IS ALWAYS SHOWING.

Is Your Attitude Helping or Hurting You in the Workplace?

Maybe your skills are not quite as good as other workers. Maybe you are not as fast or as accurate. Many times your employer and coworkers will make allowances if your attitude is good.

Also, if your attitude is good, people will like working with you. You need to think about your attitude.

STOP AND THINK

1. How is your attitude helping you on the work site? _____

_____

_____

_____

2. How is it hurting you? _____

_____

_____

_____

Give serious thought to what is happening to you in the workplace. Have you decided if your attitude is helping or hurting you? Are you satisfied with your conclusion?

Is Your Attitude Hurting You Outside the Workplace?

If your attitude is helping you in the workplace, you do not need to do this exercise. Go on to the next section.

If your attitude is hurting you in the workplace, this exercise is very important for you to do at this time. It may shed light on your problems in the workplace.

STOP AND THINK

1. Is your attitude hurting you in the workplace? Yes ___   No ___

2. If it is hurting you, what is your attitude like outside the workplace? _____

   _____

   _____

   _____

3. Does this same attitude affect the following people in your life? Check "Yes," "No," or "Maybe" for each line:

People	Yes	No	Maybe
Family			
Neighbors			
Business contacts			
Customers			

People	Yes	No	Maybe
Strangers			
Relationships			
Clerks			

4. How can you work on your attitude? What are your choices? _____

_____

_____

_____

If your attitude is hurting you in the workplace only, then maybe this is not the workplace for you. If your attitude is hurting you *in* and *outside* the workplace, then you must decide how to work on this attitude.

Everyone deals with this differently. You do have choices.

**You must deal with a bad attitude
to STAY ON THE JOB.**

Is Your Attitude Helping You Outside the Workplace?

If your attitude is helping you in the workplace, then it is probably helping you outside the workplace. You have seen the effects of a good attitude and the rewards that come with it. Do this exercise to help you keep it up.

STOP AND THINK

1. If your attitude is helping you on the work site, then analyze your attitude outside the workplace: _____

   _____

   _____

   _____

2. Does this same attitude affect the following people in your life? Check "Yes," "No," or "Maybe" for each line:

People	Yes	No	Maybe
Family			
Neighbors			
Business contacts			
Customers			
Strangers			
Relationships			
Clerks			

3. What are you doing to reinforce a positive attitude at work and outside work?

   _____

   _____

   _____

If your attitude is helping you in the workplace, then keep doing what you are doing. If it is helping you *outside* the workplace, you must *definitely* keep doing what you are doing.

Try to share with someone else who may be having a problem. It will make you a better person and a better employee.

Your Negative and Positive Feelings in the Workplace

If an attitude is your feeling toward something, and if it is an automatic response to something, then you need to know what brings on these feelings. You need to work on the good feelings and get rid of the bad feelings *because your attitude is always showing*. You need to know what creates your negative and positive feelings.

STOP AND THINK

1. Things that "tick" you off in the workplace:_____

_____

2. Words that "tick" you off in the workplace: _____

_____

3. Things that make you feel good in the workplace: _____

_____

4. Words that make you feel good in the workplace: _____

_____

All people have things that bother them and create negative feelings. If you are aware of these things and these words, you can look at the situation with a different view.

You will begin to realize that negative feelings will affect your attitude on the work site. You will begin to realize that if they affect your attitude badly, then you must fix your attitude. The bad attitude cannot last.

If there are things or words that create positive feelings, then try to use these situations to improve your attitude and remind you how to treat others.

Whether positive or negative, WHAT AFFECTS YOU WILL MOST LIKELY AFFECT OTHERS.

Fix Your Attitude

If a bad attitude is showing in the workplace, it must be worked on now. You must fix it if you want to keep your job. Most people have their own ways of fixing their attitude.

EXAMPLE

Sometimes you need a quick attitude fixer on the job site. Some fast attitude fixers are the following:

Stretch.

Take a break.

Work on something else for a while.

Look out a window.

Take a short walk.

Get a glass of water.

Go out to lunch.

Get some fresh air.

Say something nice to someone.

Volunteer to help a coworker.

STOP AND THINK

List three things that would quickly fix your attitude at work:

1. _____

2. _____

3. _____

STOP AND THINK

Doing interesting things outside of work can be an attitude fixer. Underline two things in each column that might perk you up if you were in a bad mood:

Talk to friends	Watch videos	Watch sports	Listen to music	Go to church
Play team sports	Sing	Do artwork	Do crafts	Work puzzles
Play video games	Take a walk	Ride a bike	Drive a car	Go to the city
Go to a special event	Write a letter	Write a story	Dance	Swim
Use a computer	Work out	Jog	Skate	Ski
Take a shower	Plan a trip	Party with friends	Eat in a restaurant	Snack
Go shopping	Buy something	Talk to family	Read	Play games

Now go back and compare the things you underlined. Which one of the two in each column would change your bad attitude the fastest? Circle one thing in each column that would perk you up the quickest. On the lines below, write the five things you circled:

1. _____

2. _____

3. _____

4. _____

5. _____

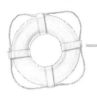
Improve Your Attitude

You know that a good attitude will get you more than a bad attitude. This is very evident in the workplace.

Your ATTITUDE, not your APTITUDE, will determine your ALTITUDE.

In other words, how you react to situations will advance you at work faster than how smart you are. If anything is worth having, it is worth working for.

You know the effects of a good attitude. You like to be with people who have a good attitude. We want our children to have a good attitude.

STOP AND THINK

You can improve your attitude and the attitudes of people around you. Name three things you can do if you need an attitude fix:

1. _____

2. _____

3. _____

Attitude is one thing you can work on and take control of. Attitude is something you cannot buy or be taught.

- Attitude is something you catch from people. If you want a good attitude, hang out with people who have good attitudes.

- If you want a good attitude, use positive words and avoid things that tick you off.

- If you want a good attitude, do some of your attitude fixers.

A good attitude will determine what you achieve on your job. A good attitude is worth working for.

CHAPTER 4

This chapter will help you

- Understand three kinds of skills.

- See the importance of skills at work.

- Discover and use your best skills.

- Improve your skills.

SKILLS

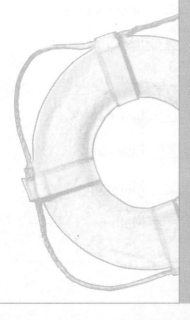

This is your SURVIVAL FOUNDATION.

You have more skills than you think you have.

You can do more than you think you can.

You are better than you think you are.

You just have to identify your skills.

This is REAL STUFF YOU NEED TO DISCOVER.

What Are Your Skills?

Skills are things you are good at or have specialized ability to do.

STOP AND THINK

Look at the following skills list. Check any skill that you think you have:

_____ Advising	_____ Evaluating
_____ Analyzing	_____ Facilitating
_____ Assessing	_____ Following directions
_____ Bookkeeping	_____ Fund-raising
_____ Budgeting	_____ Getting along
_____ Clerical	_____ Good manners
_____ Coaching	_____ Governing
_____ Communicating	_____ Human relations
_____ Computer	_____ Illustrating
_____ Conflict resolution	_____ Instructing
_____ Counseling	_____ Itemizing
_____ Creating	_____ Judging people
_____ Decision making	_____ Justifying
_____ Delegating	_____ Leading
_____ Designing	_____ Learning
_____ Diagnosing	_____ Listening
_____ Drawing	_____ Marketing
_____ Editing	_____ Math

____ Mediating		____ Reading	
____ Money making		____ Researching	
____ Motivating		____ Scheduling	
____ Music		____ Selling	
____ Nurturing		____ Singing	
____ Negotiating		____ Supervising	
____ Observing		____ Teaching	
____ Organizing		____ Training	
____ Planning		____ Typing	
____ Presenting		____ Unifying	
____ Problem solving		____ Verbalizing	
____ Public speaking		____ Writing	
____ Questioning		____ Word processing	

You have more skills than you think you have. It is just a matter of recognizing them as skills. It is just a matter of being able to explain them to someone, such as an employer. This is important when you want to improve on the job, get promoted, and find a new job.

Three Types of Skills

You need to recognize three types of skills:

- *Performance skills* are "I can" skills—things you can do.

- *Interpersonal skills* are skills you have working with people.

- *Transferable skills* are skills that can be transferred easily to various kinds of jobs.

Identify Your Performance Skills

Reminder: Performance skills are things that you can do.

EXAMPLE

Instructing or teaching is a performance skill. If you are good at instructing others, you may make a good trainer, tutor, or teacher.

STOP AND THINK

Review the skills list on pages 50-51. Select your top six performance skills. List them below:

1. _____   4. _____

2. _____   5. _____

3. _____   6. _____

Everyone has certain things that he or she can do better than the average person. Now is the time to consider what you can and have been doing.

PERFORMANCE SKILLS are part of YOUR SURVIVAL FOUNDATION.

Identify Your Interpersonal Skills

Reminder: Interpersonal skills are skills you have working with people.

EXAMPLE

The ability to communicate is an interpersonal skill. Good communication skills are important in many jobs. If you are a very good communicator, you may enjoy sales, customer service, or any job where you work with people a great deal.

STOP AND THINK

Review the skills list on pages 50-51. Select your top six interpersonal skills. List them below:

1. _____   4. _____

2. _____   5. _____

3. _____   6. _____

Are you surprised at all the skills you have? Once you have identified your skills, you can easily talk about what you can do and work on improving your skills. Skills are what you rely on to set the foundation for doing the job.

Identify Your Transferable Skills

Transferable skills can easily be transferred to most jobs. These are not necessarily specialized skills, but skills that are valuable in most work sites.

EXAMPLE

For example, organization is a skill that will easily transfer to any work site. A clerical job would require a good organizer.

STOP AND THINK

Look at your skills list on pages 50-51. Review the skills you have check marked. Which skills do you think could transfer to other jobs you would like to have? List the job on the left and your transferable skill on the right:

Job	Transferable Skill

It is important that you know which skills can easily transfer. You may be able to change job duties or take on duties that make the most of your skills. The more you know about your skills, the easier it is to talk to your current and future employers about yourself.

SKILLS give you A BETTER FOUNDATION for JOB SURVIVAL.

Another Way to Group Your Skills: Natural and Learned Skills

You may tend to pick out jobs that you think would be great, exciting, and pay good money. You do this without thinking about the skills required to be good at that particular job.

You think you can do the job and just plunge into it. You discover later that you can do the job. *But* you cannot be good at it, and you do not like the job anymore.

STOP AND THINK

Review your skills list on pages 50-51. Which skills do you think came naturally (you were born with) and which do you think were learned or developed? Put an "N" by the skills that came naturally. Put an "L" by the skills you have learned.

Now list your top six natural and top six learned skills:

Natural

1. _____   4. _____

2. _____   5. _____

3. _____   6. _____

Learned

1. _____   4. _____

2. _____   5. _____

3. _____   6. _____

Why is it you want to spend time trying jobs that require skills that are difficult for you? If they are difficult for you, you will not stay on the job. You must stop and think.

Begin to recognize your NATURAL SKILLS and your best LEARNED SKILLS.

Your natural skills are your strongest skills. These are skills that will allow you to be exceptional in your job.

Your next best skills are your easily learned skills. They can also carry you to the top.

Give these skills respect, and you strengthen your JOB SURVIVAL foundation.

Know Your Natural Skills

Your natural skills are skills you were born with. These are your natural abilities and talents. These are your gifts. If developed and perfected, they will allow you to do great things on jobs that require these skills.

EXAMPLE

Joy loved to design things on paper when she was a child. She would spend hours designing cars, furniture, toys, clothes, and houses.

Joy chose a job with a manufacturing company. All manufacturing companies have design departments. Joy did very well in this company. She has a natural skill, which helped her advance rapidly.

Know your NATURAL SKILLS.

STOP AND THINK

Review carefully your natural skills list on page 55. List them 1 through 6, with 1 being your strongest. Then answer the questions.

Natural Skills

1. _____

2. _____ Would you rather do 1 or 2? _____

3. _____ Would you rather do 1 or 3? _____

4. _____ Would you rather do 1 or 4? _____

5. _____ Would you rather do 1 or 5? _____

6. _____ Would you rather do 1 or 6? _____

Would you rather do 2 or 3? _____

Would you rather do 2 or 4? _____

Would you rather do 2 or 5? _____

Would you rather do 2 or 6? _____

Would you rather do 3 or 4? _____

Would you rather do 3 or 5? _____

Would you rather do 3 or 6? _____

Would you rather do 4 or 5? _____

Would you rather do 4 or 6? _____

Would you rather do 5 or 6? _____

(continues)

(continued)

Look at your answers:

How many "1"s do you have? _____

How many "2"s do you have? _____

How many "3"s do you have? _____

How many "4"s do you have? _____

How many "5"s do you have? _____

How many "6"s do you have? _____

What number do you have the most of? _____

What would you most like to do with this skill? _____

_____

_____

Now you know your number 1 natural skill. Try to use it. If you seek out jobs that require your natural skills, you have the opportunity to be the best at the job.

You will do better at jobs you like doing, and how lucky you are if the skills come naturally.

Know Your Best Learned Skills

It is important that you know your best learned skills when looking for your next job or promotion. If you can take a job that requires these skills, you have the advantage over others applying for the job. This is a skill you have already learned well.

A learned skill can come from many places, including other jobs, school, self-teaching, a hobby, or from being taught by someone else. Try to utilize this skill.

EXAMPLE

Richard was given an old car when he turned 16. He loved the car, but it was always breaking down. Richard's parents would not pay for repairs. Richard started learning how to do his own repairs. He bought parts and tools and did all the mechanical work himself.

Richard became a great mechanic. He took a job in the airplane industry working on planes. He did very well because he used his learned skills.

Know your LEARNED SKILLS.

STOP AND THINK

Review carefully your learned skills list on page 55. List them 1 through 6, with 1 being your strongest. Then answer the questions.

Learned Skills

1. _____

2. _____ Would you rather do 1 or 2? _____

3. _____ Would you rather do 1 or 3? _____

4. _____ Would you rather do 1 or 4? _____

5. _____ Would you rather do 1 or 5? _____

6. _____ Would you rather do 1 or 6? _____

Would you rather do 2 or 3? _____

Would you rather do 2 or 4? _____

(continues)

(continued)

Would you rather do 2 or 5? _____

Would you rather do 2 or 6? _____

Would you rather do 3 or 4? _____

Would you rather do 3 or 5? _____

Would you rather do 3 or 6? _____

Would you rather do 4 or 5? _____

Would you rather do 4 or 6? _____

Would you rather do 5 or 6? _____

Look at your answers:

How many "1"s do you have? _____

How many "2"s do you have? _____

How many "3"s do you have? _____

How many "4"s do you have? _____

How many "5"s do you have? _____

How many "6"s do you have? _____

What number do you have the most of? _____

What would you most like to do with this skill? _____

_____

_____

Now you know your number 1 learned skill. Try to use it.

It is much easier to take a job that requires skills you already have. It makes the job more secure and exciting. Although you may need to learn other skills, your job survival foundation is safer if you have the skills required to do your job.

Put Your Skills to Work

Keep in your head your natural and learned skills when reading job descriptions. Look carefully at the requirements. Stop and think: Do I have these skills? Is this job description a natural for me? Have I learned these skills? Do I like using them?

STOP AND THINK

Circle anything that will use your number 1 natural skill. Box anything that will use your number 1 learned skill.

Accounting	Guiding	Judging
Financing	Hair	Computers
Nature	Automotive	Cooking
Assembling	Helping others	Customer relations
Follow through	Building	Decision making
Negotiating	Human relations	Leading
Administrative	Buying	Delegating
Getting along	Instructing	Reporting
Analyzing	Care-giving	Marketing
Bookkeeping	Cleaning	Drawing
Budgeting	Itemizing	Math
Grooming	Clerical	Selling

(continues)

(continued)

Measuring	Presenting	Singing
Enforcing	Problem solving	Supervising
Teaching	Public speaking	Managing
Explaining	Listening	Traveling
Nursing	Researching	Typing
Word processing	Scheduling	Verbalizing
Performing	Employing	Organizing
Plants	Servicing	Writing

The list gives you familiar words found in job descriptions and job ads. You need to think about these words and associate them with your natural and learned skills.

Start thinking about jobs that require your skills. You can find out about jobs that require your skills in many ways. Some ideas include the following:

- Read job ads.

- Talk to people who have jobs that interest you.

- Do library and Internet research.

It is important that you know which jobs could require your skills.

You have to do your homework and take control of your JOB SURVIVAL FOUNDATION.

Fields of Employment That Would Use Your Skills

If you are good at writing and have writing skills, what types of jobs would require or prefer good writing skills? What fields of work could you enter? You must start thinking about job fields.

STOP AND THINK

List six things you have circled on pages 61-62 that use your number 1 natural skill:

1. _____   4. _____

2. _____   5. _____

3. _____   6. _____

List six things you have boxed on pages 61-62 that use your number 1 learned skill:

1. _____   4. _____

2. _____   5. _____

3. _____   6. _____

If you have a job that does not use your natural or learned skills, think of fields of work that could use these skills. Once you identify these fields, then you can start thinking of specific jobs that may fit you better.

You now begin to realize how to emphasize these skills on a job application, for a promotion, or in everyday conversation.

Specific Jobs That Would Use Your Skills

Once you start identifying jobs in certain job fields, you will start to see where your skills fit. You will begin to realize how quickly an advertisement for a job can specify required skills in very few words.

STOP AND THINK

List the six things from page 63 that use your natural skill.

Write the field that this work would fall under in the middle column and a job you can go for on the right. Be specific about jobs where people who are good in this category are hired.

Example: Word—*singing*. Field—*music*. Job—*music store sales*.

Word Associated with Your Natural Skill	Field of Work	Specific Job
1.		
2.		
3.		
4.		
5.		
6.		

Now do the same thing for your learned skill:

Example: Word—*plants*. Field—*gardening*. Job—*landscape worker*.

Word Associated with Your Learned Skill	Field of Work	Specific Job
1.		
2.		
3.		
4.		
5.		
6.		

Jobs can be entry-level jobs in the field. Jobs can give you experience and advance you in that field. Jobs can give you the opportunity to display your best skills.

Know the SKILLS that can SECURE YOUR JOB.

Study Newspaper Advertisements

Learning to read a newspaper advertisement is good practice for anyone who is working or going to work. Ads are short and to the point.

They tell you what skills are needed for specific jobs. They also get you familiar with job titles and what skills are required. You can learn a lot about the workplace from job advertisements.

STOP AND THINK

Read the following advertisements. Using your skills list as a guide, list beside each ad what skills you think it would take to do the job:

Skills

Associate Designer. Dynamic and fast-growing women's and men's sportswear company needs creative, idea-oriented designer. Must be a self-starting, well-disciplined individual w/a desire to excel. Sportswear experience preferred. Required computer skills: MS Office, Excel, and CAD. Fax resume to 555-000-0000.

_____

_____

_____

_____

_____

Skills

PAYROLL. Accounting Asst. needed to handle payroll and A/R in high-volume office. PR: multi/division, prev. wage. A/R: invoicing, lien procedures, exp. data entry. Mas 90 helpful. Must be able to handle multiple tasks. Mail or fax resume to E & E Roofing, P.O. Box 0000, Anytown, CA 00000.

_____

_____

_____

_____

_____

(continues)

(continued)

SALES MANAGER

National operator of manufactured housing communities seeking professional sales manager. Successful candidate must possess strong sales, marketing, and management abilities. Real estate sales license not required. Excellent compensation package. For immediate consideration, please fax your resume to D. Smith, 555-000-0000.

Skills

_____

_____

_____

_____

_____

MANAGEMENT TEAM

Stop Commuting! Friendly, mature individuals needed who enjoy meeting the public. Excellent training & benefits for self-motivated, enthusiastic couple. This is a resident manager position in a brand new facility. Fax resume with cover letter to James, (555) 000-0000, or mail to 111 Main St., Anytown, NY 00000.

Skills

_____

_____

_____

_____

_____

SALES

Inside Admissions Rep. Small pvt. college seeking an Inside Student Recruiter. Candidate must be prof., enthusiastic, with strong people skills. Indiv. must be driven to meet, exceed budgeted goals. Sales & telemarketing exp. recommended. Fax resume to Michael: 555-000-0000. EOE

Skills

_____

_____

_____

_____

_____

Skills

_____

Bookkeeper: Good computer skills needed. Great working environment. Prof. appearance. (555) 000-0000.

_____

_____

_____

_____

The more familiar you are with skills required for specific jobs, the better you know how to approach the job market. You will know how to match your skills with a job, how to talk quickly about your skills, and how to market your skills to an employer. You will do a better job if you use your skills. Always know what skills it will take to survive on the job.

Use Your Strongest Natural and Learned Skills

Knowing and using your natural gifted skill is the easiest, most rewarding, and most beneficial way to do your best work. If perfected, it can carry you to the top level of your job or career.

Knowing and using your best learned skill can also bring you to the top level of your job. Remember, performance is a must on the work site.

STOP AND THINK

1. Your strongest natural skill: _____

2. When did you discover you had this skill? _____

   _____

3. Your strongest learned skill: _____

4. When did you learn this skill? _____

   _____

You should take advantage of your NATURAL SKILL. It is a gift.

You should take advantage of your LEARNED SKILL. It is an accomplishment.

(continues)

(continued)

5. Describe one job or career where you could use both skills if you were asked to start tomorrow: _____

_____

_____

GO for IT.

Improve Your Skills

Understanding your skills, where they come from, how they were acquired, and how to use them is very important in the workplace. Recognizing your skill strengths and weaknesses puts you ahead in the workplace.

If your skills are strong, go for a job that uses your strong skills. Look for ways to use your best skills in the job you have now. If your skills are weak, improve them.

Some ways to improve both your strong and weak skills are the following:

- Learn through on-the-job training.
- Go back to school.
- Take specialized courses and seminars.
- Read, do research, and study.
- Take up a new hobby.
- Do volunteer work.
- Get entry-level work experience.

A reminder: A natural skill is a gift—use it if possible. A learned skill is an accomplishment—use it if possible.

You must develop a strong
JOB FOUNDATION to survive on the job.

CHAPTER 5

This chapter will help you

- Plan short-term goals.

- Plan long-term goals.

- Motivate yourself to reach your goals.

GOALS

This is your SURVIVAL MAP.

Goals are important to keep you focused.

Goals point you in the direction that you want to be moving.

Want to achieve something in the next week, month, or year? Set a goal to get you there.

It is said, "A goal is a dream with a deadline."

This is STUFF YOU NEED TO TAKE TIME TO DO.

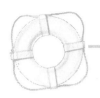
Plan a Trip Step-by-Step

Goals keep you focused. Goals put you in the right direction. Goals help you get moving to where you want to go.

EXAMPLE

Do you want to get to work on time? Do you want to learn a new computer program? Do you want to make more money? Set a goal! Goals will help your job survival.

Setting goals is like planning a trip. One step at a time, you keep your vision on your final destination.

STOP AND THINK

You have three weeks of vacation time. Pick a destination you would like to see—someplace that would take two or three days to reach by car.

Destination: _____

List the steps you have to take to get ready for this trip:

1. _____

2. _____

3. _____

4. _____

5. _____

6. _____

What do you have to consider before taking these steps?

1. _____

2. _____

3. _____

4. _____

5. _____

6. _____

When planning a trip, you must decide the following:

- Your destination.

- How long it will take to get there.

- How you will get there.

- What you need to take with you.

- What the cost will be.

- Where you have to be the first night, the second night, and so on.

- What you will do when you get there.

- How long you can stay.

SETTING a GOAL is much THE SAME.

Visualize Your Trip

Try to visualize every step of your trip. Visualize arriving at your destination. This will help you to organize your steps.

STOP AND THINK

Draw a picture of your trip. For example, you can draw roads taken, meals eaten, sights seen, and hotels stayed at.

Day one:

Day two:

Final destination:

Visualize what you are going for. It is a great motivator. It keeps you focused.

Your final DESTINATION is the REWARD.
Goals are your SURVIVAL MAP.

STOP AND THINK

Imagine you have reached your destination. Was the trip worthwhile? Did you get tired or discouraged? Did you enjoy the day-by-day traveling? Was the payoff as good as you hoped? Was the payoff worth it? _____

_____

_____

_____

Plan Short-Term and Long-Term Goals

Short-term goals are those that you want to reach in the near future: next week, next month, or in six months. Long-term goals are those that will take longer to reach.

EXAMPLE

Short-term goals can be achievements in themselves, such as learning a new task at work.

Short-term goals also can be made to reach long-term goals. An example is taking classes (short-term goals) you need to get a diploma (long-term goal).

Short-term goals that are planned well will keep you moving toward your long-term goals.

For any goal, visualize the steps needed to reach it. Just like planning your trip, visualize the first steps first. Make a plan. Try to determine what each step will bring. Each step can be a short-term goal.

STOP AND THINK

Setting goals is like planning a trip. Do you have goals? Why or why not? _____

_____

_____

_____

Determine one destination. It can be short-term or long-term: _____

_____

What steps do you have to take to start your plan?

1. _____

2. _____

3. _____

4. _____

5. _____

6. _____

What do you have to consider before taking these steps?

1. _____

2. _____

3. _____

4. _____

5. _____

6. _____

Planning can be the most important part in reaching your goals. Be sure to plan for your job survival.

Look at Career Goals

You can use goal planning to create a career plan. To help you think about planning your career, pretend that you are a career advisor.

This will help you plan steps for a successful career. You will consider steps more carefully when advising someone else.

STOP AND THINK

Imagine that people of all ages come to you for career advice. It is your job to help them create a successful career.

1. Dana has not worked in 10 years but thinks she would like to be a nurse. What advice would you give her? (Hint: You might suggest that she volunteer at a hospital, talk to nurses, and do research on nursing.): _____

   _____

   _____

2. John likes trucks. He used to deliver building materials before he got into trouble with the law. His driver's license has expired. He is not sure about his driving record. What advice would you give him?_____

   _____

   _____

Giving career advice to someone else is a big responsibility. You must weigh your advice against the person's situation.

You should do the same for yourself when thinking about your goals.

STOP AND THINK

Consider the following people's needs and desires carefully before giving advice. What short-term goal will it take to reach the long-term goal?

1. Jane dropped out of school several years ago. Jane thinks she would like to be a teacher, but she is not quite sure. What advice would you give her? _____

   _____

   _____

2. Jose has been in this country one year, but he has not mastered English. He speaks Spanish at home and with his friends. He would like to eventually manage a restaurant. What advice would you give him? _____

_____

_____

When giving advice, consider whether you think the long-term goal is reachable for this person. If it is reachable, what steps should be taken to reach a short-term goal? What steps should be taken to reach the long-term goal?

Do this for yourself in setting goals at work, in your career, and in your personal life.

Then follow your SURVIVAL MAP.

Set Your Career Goals

STOP AND THINK

Ask yourself two questions before setting short-term and long-term career goals:

- What do you want to do as a career or job?

- What do you want your career to do for you?

Write your ideal career: _____

_____

(continues)

(continued)

Now list all the things you want this career to do for you. Examples: Buy new clothes. Make me independent. Send my kids to college. _____

_____

_____

_____

_____

_____

_____

What goals can you set to make all these things happen? Think of everything. Ideas include trying harder at work, getting extra training, saving money, getting a promotion, learning something new at work, getting a family member to help with housework, and so on. Write these goals below:

6 Months	12 Months	5 Years

Chart Other Goals

The table below lists some areas to think about for goal making. For each item listed down the side, think about where you want to be in 6 months, 12 months, and 5 years. These are your goals.

STOP AND THINK

Where do you want to be in 6 months? How do you want to be getting to work in 12 months? How much money will you be making in 5 years? List your goals beside each item in the columns below.

Item	6 Months	12 Months	5 Years
Location			
Housing			
Transportation			
Finances			
Relationships			
Health			
Education			
Other Goals			

Be sure to think of all the steps needed to reach your goals. Job survival can help you reach these other goals.

Have You Always Reached Your Goals?

Sometimes it is easier to succeed if you can look back on a time you failed. When you think about something you did not succeed in, you can see the reasons for your failure. You can correct it the next time.

STOP AND THINK

1. Is there something you tried to accomplish but did not succeed? Yes ___ No ___

   Please explain: _____

   _____

2. Do you know why you did not succeed? _____

   _____

   _____

3. If you could do it over, what would you do differently? _____

   _____

   _____

4. Describe what you tried to do: _____

   _____

   _____

5. What was the goal? _____

   _____

6. What steps did you fail to take that destroyed your goal? _____

   _____

   _____

7. How did you feel when you did not reach your goal? _____

   _____

   _____

Learning through failure can be very powerful. It can be a lasting learning experience.

It can help you correct mistakes and remind you not to make them again.

LEARNING from the past creates SUCCESS.

Think About Past Success

Is there something you have done that you are very proud of? Were you the main person responsible for something's success?

EXAMPLE

The successful activity could be going to work every day on time, giving a party, raising a child, completing a job assignment, running a church event, refinishing a table, or training a dog. It does not have to be big—just successful.

STOP AND THINK

1. Describe the accomplishment: _____

_____

2. What was the goal? _____

_____

3. What steps did it take to accomplish the goal? _____

_____

_____

(continues)

(continued)

> 4. How did it feel when you reached the goal? _____
>
> _____

It is important that you think of a successful accomplishment. Remind yourself of your plan and the steps you took to reach this goal. Repeat this exercise over and over and over.

Motivate Yourself

Without motivation, there is no reason to try to reach a goal.

EXAMPLE

A farmer had a workhorse that he needed to work his fields. Without this horse, the farmer could not plow, plant, or harvest his fields.

Like many horses, this horse did not want to work every day. So the farmer needed to motivate the horse to work every day.

Fortunately, the horse liked carrots. So the farmer tied a carrot on a stick and held it in front of the horse's nose.

The carrot had to be just the right distance from the nose. It could not be close enough for the horse to eat. But the horse still had to see and smell it. The dangled carrot kept the horse moving, always thinking he could reach the carrot.

People have "carrots" too. Some carrots might be more money, self-respect, a nicer place to live, helping someone, better health, learning something new, a car, a vacation, or a feeling of accomplishment. All of these could be your job survival "carrots."

STOP AND THINK

1. What carrots could motivate you? _____

_____

_____

_____

_____

2. Will these carrots keep you moving? Yes ___ No ___

   Please explain: _____

   _____

3. Are they carrots that you are willing to work every day to get? Yes ___ No ___

   Please explain: _____

   _____

4. Review your list from question 1. Which four carrots would take you straight to your biggest goal?

   _____

   _____

   _____

   _____

Even a horse has to have a reason to work. You must be motivated to reach a goal or to keep a job.

Know what motivates you. Is it strong enough to keep you on the job and to reach your goal?

What You Want Your Goals to Do for You

You know your goals. You know the steps needed to reach your goals. You know what will motivate you to pursue your goals. You have done a complete self-assessment.

STOP AND THINK

List everything you expect your goals to do for you:

1. _____

2. _____

3. _____

4. _____

5. _____

6. _____

7. _____

8. _____

9. _____

10. _____

Look at your list. Wouldn't this be great? If you do not know where you are going and the steps to take, you will not get there. Goal setting is necessary for successful employment and job survival. It is your map. It will determine your job destination.

Like all maps, you must FOLLOW IT CLOSELY. Follow your SURVIVAL MAP.

CHAPTER 6

This chapter will help you

- Solve problems through time management.

- Solve problems through possibility thinking.

- Nip small problems before they grow.

- Make backup plans.

- Find people to discuss your problems with.

PROBLEM SOLVING

This is your SURVIVAL CHALLENGE.

Employers say problem solving seems hard for those who have not worked much or for those who are reentering the workplace.

You face both work and personal problems. Sometimes these problems overlap or affect each other.

If you can solve your problems, you help your job survival.

This is STUFF YOU HAVE TO SOLVE.

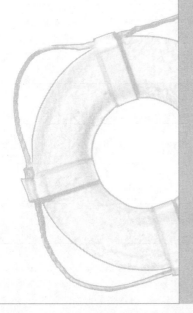

Problems at Work and in Life

Everyone has problems to solve in life. Everyone has different problems to solve.

What may be a problem for one person may not be a problem for you. People do not see things in the same way.

Learning how to solve problems will help you survive your job and move ahead in life. This chapter will show you some problem-solving methods.

Method I: Use Time Management

Learning how to manage your time will help you prevent or solve many problems. Many problems are related to time management.

The first step is to know what tasks you personally have to do in your working day. Many work issues that arise are personal issues getting in the way of work.

Time management, like money management, is not something that comes naturally. It is something you have to work at to get the most results.

STOP AND THINK

Start by reviewing your priorities and values from Chapter 2. List all the things that will require good time management in your workweek. Child care is one example.

1. _____

2. _____

3. _____

4. _____

5. _____

6. _____

7. _____

8. _____

9. _____

10. _____

11. _____

12. _____

13. _____

14. _____

15. _____

Unless you are aware of what needs to be managed in your workweek, you are probably creating a problem that will show up on the work site. You cannot let problems go that will affect the work site. Now is the time to take your list seriously.

Where Does Your Time Go?

We are all different. But one thing is the same for everyone, no matter what your sex, age, race, health, education level, finances, or background.

Everyone has seven days in a week. Everyone has 24 hours in a day. Everyone has 168 hours in a week. You have a choice in how you spend these hours.

This is called TIME MANAGEMENT.

 STOP AND THINK

Look at the list on pages 86-87 of things to manage in your life. List them and the time you allot to do these things:

(continues)

(continued)

Things to Manage	Time Allotted
1.	
2.	
3.	
4.	
5.	
6.	
7.	
8.	
9.	
10.	
11.	
12.	
13.	
14.	
15.	

Most people never make a list of tasks to be managed in their lives. Many people think about it but never write it down to review every now and then.

TIME MANAGEMENT IS A MUST
to fix problems related to your job.

Look at Your Time Use

Have you ever thought about how many hours and minutes you have in a week? Most persons have not. It is good to know *where* you spend time and *how* you spend your time. It could solve some problems.

STOP AND THINK

Look at your list on page 88. Count the total time it takes to do everything on your list.

1. Total time allotted: _____

2. Is it under 168 hours? Yes ____   No ____

3. Is it over 168 hours? Yes ____   No ____

4. Do you think you can do everything in one week? Yes ____   No ____

   If no, are there tasks you can do every other week? Yes ____   No ____ List these tasks: _____

   _____

   _____

5. Can you share some tasks with someone else? Yes ____   No ____ List these tasks:

   _____

   _____

(continues)

(continued)

6. Can you do some tasks in less time? Yes ___ No ___ List these tasks: _____

_____

_____

7. Do you have any time left for yourself and for activities like sleeping and eating?
Yes ___ No ___

Looking at how and where your weekly time is spent helps you make needed changes. Your working life demands certain hours. Do you have issues that disturb your working hours? Solve them *immediately* if you want to survive on the job.

Solving problems is a CHALLENGE.

Free Up Some Time in Your Week

Time management can help you avoid conflicts on the work site.

EXAMPLE

An example is when you need to get to the bank. You need to take care of banking needs when you are not at work. You must have flexible hours in your week. These hours are not set for specific things.

Your job hours are a specific thing. Your job requires set hours that are *not* flexible. Unexpected things will come up and require time in your week. You must anticipate these issues and solve the problem.

Stop and Think

Look at your list on page 88.

1. What can you give up doing? _____

_____

2. What can you spend less time doing? _____

_____

3. Redo your list below and try to free up a few hours:

	Things to Manage	Time Allotted
1.		
2.		
3.		
4.		
5.		
6.		
7.		
8.		
9.		
10.		

(continues)

(continued)

Things to Manage	Time Allotted
11.	
12.	
13.	
14.	
15.	

You cannot do everything on your list when you work a job. The job demands a certain number of hours that were yours to spend before going to work.

You also need time for yourself. It doesn't have to be a long period, but it must be your time. It is healthy for your working week.

It will not be easy to readjust your time. But it has to be done. This list will help you to adjust or eliminate certain things to be managed.

This is PROBLEM SOLVING, and IT IS A CHALLENGE.

Method 2: Use Possibility Thinking

Problem solving requires possibility thinking. Possibility thinking is another way to solve problems.

When you have a problem, ask yourself: "What are the possible solutions for this problem?"

Also ask, "Am I part of the problem or am I part of the solution?"

EXAMPLE

Mary has been clocking in late at work. The bus she takes does not arrive in front of her work until 9:01. She is scheduled to start work at 9 a.m. Her coworkers are grumbling. The boss is not pleased.

Mary always blames the bus for her problem. But with possibility thinking, she lists the following ways to solve her problem:

- Take an earlier bus.

- Take a different bus and walk four blocks.

- Get a ride with a coworker.

- Have a family member or neighbor drop me off.

- Move closer to work.

- Ask my boss if I can change my work hours.

STOP AND THINK

1. Daniel is a front-desk receptionist at a temporary placement firm. He is responsible for 17 telephone lines. There have been complaints about him forgetting names and hitting the wrong extensions.

   Is Daniel part of the problem? Yes ___ No ___

   How can he use possibility thinking? _____

   _____

   _____

2. Jackson is a hotshot salesperson. He prides himself on being able to close a sale. He has always been one of the top salespersons in his company. Calling possible

(continues)

(continued)

> customers is a must in his business. Jackson does not like the phone and recognized it when first taking the job. Jackson hired a person to make his appointments and do his telephoning for him.
>
> Is Jackson part of the problem or the solution? _____
>
> How did he use possibility thinking? _____
>
> _____
>
> _____

Every work-related problem has a possible solution. When it is a problem for you, consider every way to solve the problem.

You must be honest about your part in the problem. Is the problem created because of something you did or did not do? Is the problem something you were brought in to solve?

Practice POSSIBILITY THINKING.

How Home and Work Affect Each Other

When you are solving work-related problems, it may be difficult to separate work and home problems because they often affect each other.

Many of these problems are related to time management. Many are related to prioritizing. Many are communication problems. But possibility thinking will help you for all problems.

All PROBLEMS have to be SOLVED.

EXAMPLE

Jane was working overtime several days a week. Jane wanted the money and was afraid she would lose her job if she refused to work overtime. Jane's husband did not like her to work overtime and started spending time in the local bar. How does Jane need to solve this problem?

Jane's list of possibilities included the following: Ask if I can work overtime on Saturday morning. Ask if I can work extra time before regular starting hours. Ask if I can take some work home with me. Explain all my concerns to my husband. Find another job.

STOP AND THINK

Jason's wife had a doctor's appointment on Wednesday at 10:30 a.m. She did not drive, so Jason had to take her to the appointment. Jason was an accounting clerk but decided it was not important for him to go to work that morning since he was taking his wife to the doctor.

During the morning, one of his largest customers complained about an account discrepancy. Jason had the books at home, so the company could not correct the problem. The company could not get in touch with Jason. The company lost the account.

How does Jason need to solve the problem? _____

_____

_____

When home and work problems begin to affect each other, it is time to do some serious possibility thinking. The problem demands immediate attention. You must find the root of the problem.

Problems will affect JOB SURVIVAL.
They are a CHALLENGE.

Method 3: Solve Small Problems Before They Grow

Small problems can grow into large problems if you let them. A small problem at home can create large problems at work. A small problem at work can turn into large problems at home. Solving small problems is easier than solving large problems.

Small problems can get bigger. They can get bigger *fast*. It does not matter if they start at home or work. They can create problems at both places if they are not stopped. Think of all the small problems at either place that can grow large very rapidly.

STOP AND THINK

Write down small problems at home that could turn into large problems at work:

1. _____

2. _____

3. _____

4. _____

5. _____

Write down small problems at work that could turn into large problems at home:

1. _____

2. _____

3. _____

4. _____

5. _____

Write down small problems at work that could turn into large problems at work:

1. _____

2. _____

3. _____

4. _____

5. _____

Foresight is better than hindsight. Try to anticipate small problems that could change fast. Take care of these small problems as they occur.

Do NOT IGNORE SMALL PROBLEMS.
They can affect your job survival.

Method 4: Make a Backup Plan

People do not always foresee problems. You certainly do not want to start creating problems.

You do know certain issues create common problems for people who work. Consider these and other problems. Then make a backup plan. This is another problem-solving method.

STOP AND THINK

Here are three common problems that occur at home and affect a person's working day. What would be your backup plan if these were your small problems at your home?

(continues)

(continued)

Problem	Backup Plan
Child care	
Transportation	
Doctor's appointment	

Here are three common problems that occur at work and affect people at home. What would be your backup plan if these were your small problems at work?

Problem	Backup Plan
Clocking in late	
Lack of updated clothing	
Calling home frequently	

Your backup plan is very important. People who work have times when they cannot do their best work because something interferes. Some problems are common and require a backup plan from the start of your job. Other problems may come and go, but you still need a backup plan.

Method 5: Talk About Your Problems

Problems will always come up at work and at home. They may be small problems, or small problems that can turn into large problems. It is good if you have someone you can discuss the problem with. This is another problem-solving technique.

Problems at Work

When problems arise in the workplace, it is important to choose someone to share the problem with. This must be someone you trust to keep it between the two of you. This must be someone you trust to give good advice.

It helps to clear your thinking and get another opinion. You do not want to carry these problems outside the workplace. Try to leave them at work.

A good practice: INSIDE PROBLEMS—KEEP INSIDE.

STOP AND THINK

1. Do you have someone to talk with at work? Yes ___ No ___

2. Describe this person or the person you would like to approach if necessary:

   _____

3. Why this person? _____

   _____

Remember: Inside problems—kept inside.

If you talk to someone, you can reenergize and have a clearer picture of the problem. You will make better decisions than if you have fussed about the problem after leaving the work site. Carrying work problems home does nothing for job survival.

Problems at Home

Home problems should not be carried to work. You cannot do your best work if you are thinking about problems at home. You know this is not always possible. But it will help if you have someone outside of work to share and discuss problems with.

Remember the practice: OUTSIDE PROBLEMS—KEEP OUTSIDE.

When problems arise at home that you foresee affecting your work life, you need to choose a person with whom you can confide. This should be someone who will give you good advice. This should be someone you can trust to keep it between the two of you.

STOP AND THINK

1. Do you have someone to talk with about problems at home? Yes ___ No ___

2. Describe this person or the person you would like to approach if necessary:

   _____

3. Why this person? _____

   _____

Remember: Outside problems—kept outside.

Practice this exercise. Make it a practice that you try very hard to always do. Taking home problems to the work site is more threatening to your job than carrying work problems home.

This is why choosing someone to talk to outside work is so important. People at work do not want to hear or be involved in your home problems. It spells trouble for you. This is very critical to your job survival.

Problem solving is a BIG SURVIVAL CHALLENGE.

CHAPTER 7

This chapter will help you

- Recognize your good and bad habits.

- See the effects of habits in your work life.

- See the effects of habits in your personal life.

- Change bad habits and have more good habits.

HABITS

This is your
SURVIVAL GUIDE.

It is hard to recognize
your own habits.

Habits are so much a
part of you that you do not see
them as habits.

You do not see their effects on
your working life. Do not
underestimate the effects of
good and bad habits.

This STUFF
BELONGS TO YOU.

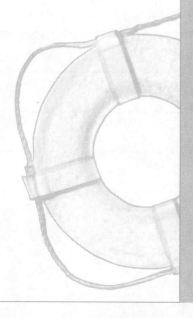

Recognize Your Good Habits

Habits are constant, often unconscious, behavior patterns acquired by frequent repetition. You need to recognize what in your daily life has become a habit (an often-unconscious repetition).

Habits can be good or bad. Good habits play an important role in keeping a job. Bad habits play an important role in losing a job.

EXAMPLE

You know when a habit is good if it has improved your work life or performance in some way. For example, a good habit is making a to-do list to stay organized. Other good habits are being on time, being neat, and finishing your work on time.

STOP AND THINK

List all the good habits you do during your daily or weekly routine. Start with when you get up in the morning:

1. _____

2. _____

3. _____

4. _____

5. _____

6. _____

7. _____

8. _____

9. _____

10. _____

11. _____

12. _____

13. _____

14. _____

15. _____

16. _____

17. _____

18. _____

19. _____

20. _____

Knowing and continuing your daily good habits can make a big difference on the work site. If good habits are improving you and what you do, then they are improving your job performance.

GOOD HABITS are a GOOD job survival GUIDE.

Recognize Your Bad Habits

Habits are constant, often unconscious, behavior patterns acquired by frequent repetition.

It may be easier to see your bad habits, since they are more readily brought to your attention. Bad habits will play a part in your job performance.

 EXAMPLE

You know when a habit is bad if it makes you or what you are doing look bad. For example, being late is a bad habit. Other bad habits are sloppy work, making excuses, and waiting until the last minute to start something.

STOP AND THINK

List all the bad habits you do during your daily or weekly routine. Start with when you get up in the morning:

1. _____

2. _____

3. _____

4. _____

5. _____

6. _____

7. _____

8. _____

9. _____

10. _____

11. _____

12. _____

13. _____

14. _____

15. _____

16. _____

17. _____

18. _____

19. _____

20. _____

You need to recognize what in your daily life has become a bad habit (an unconscious repetition). If habits are not improving you or what you do, then they are hurting you on the job or elsewhere. Bad habits can hurt job performance and job survival. You need a survival guide.

Develop Good Habits

You know by observation or experience that good habits are great to develop early in life. You may not have developed these habits yourself, but as a teacher or parent, you would encourage them. Why? Because you know good habits are an advantage to you in life.

STOP AND THINK

You are a fourth-grade teacher. The children are 9 and 10 years old. What habits would you encourage them to develop early in their lives?

Good Habit	Why Would You Encourage It?

(continues)

(continued)

Good Habit	Why Would You Encourage It?

Good habits work and should be formed early in life. If you recognize how good habits work for you, then you can start now trying to develop these habits.

It will not be easy, but you can develop good working habits that will improve your job performance.

Discourage Bad Habits

You would discourage a child from forming bad habits. Why would you do this as a teacher or a parent? You know bad habits will hurt the child if he or she continues to do them.

 ## STOP AND THINK

You are a fourth-grade teacher. The children are 9 and 10 years old. What habits would you discourage them from continuing?

Bad Habit	Why Would You Discourage It?

Bad habits will hurt you if you do not work on changing them. If you would discourage a child from continuing bad habits, then why not work on your own bad habits?

BAD HABITS can INTERFERE with your JOB PERFORMANCE.

Self-Test: Your Sixth-Grade Habits

Habits—good or bad—that you form early in life are difficult to change. You carry them right into adulthood in everything you do. You carry them into the workplace and apply them on the work site.

STOP AND THINK

1. When you were in the sixth grade, what were your habits?

Habit	Yes	No
Always to school on time		
Made excuses for not going to school		
Always got homework in on time		
Homework always neat		
Got along with classmates		
Asked questions when not understanding		
Used four-letter words with friends		
Listened to teachers and classmates		
Got good night's sleep before tests		
Conformed to school dress code		
Gave excuses for late homework		
Blamed others for things gone wrong		
Procrastinated		
Careless in homework		
Last-minute person		

Habit	Yes	No
Well-organized person		
Fast reader		
Read lots of books		
Good at math		
Was a leader		
Was a follower		
Good problem solver		
Liked to speak in front of class		
Liked team playing		
Had lots of friends		
Few friends		
A loner		
Social butterfly		
Temperamental		
Stubborn		
Had lots of hobbies		
Selfish		
Gossip/tattletale		

(continues)

(continued)

2. What patterns do you see in your habits? _____

_____

_____

3. What good and bad habits are you still doing? _____

_____

_____

4. What habits have you improved since sixth grade? _____

_____

_____

5. What habits could apply to your work life? _____

_____

_____

Can you SURVIVE the JOB with THESE HABITS?

Baggage You Carry in Your Personal Life

People will try to change bad habits when these habits start to make them look bad. It is not easy to break a bad habit. You will usually justify or make excuses that it is not a bad habit.

The best way to admit a bad habit is to look at the effect it has on your life. Was it a bad effect? Then it was a bad habit.

Take a look at your sixth-grade list. Are you still carrying bad habits with you? This is called *baggage*. It can be heavy and weigh you down.

STOP AND THINK

List the bad habits and how they have affected your personal life:

Bad Habit	Effect on Personal Life

If a bad habit has affected you in your personal life, you have to determine how bad it was for you. If this habit has always caused you problems, then you have to work on it. If it is a habit you have had since childhood, try to understand why.

You can BREAK a BAD HABIT.

Baggage You Carry to the Work Site

If you are carrying bad habits to the work site, you need to know how they affect your work performance. You need to know how they affect your work image. You need to be aware of how you look to other employees and coworkers.

Take a look at your sixth-grade list. Are you still carrying bad habits around? This is called *baggage*. It can be heavy and weigh you down.

STOP AND THINK

List the bad habits and how they have affected your work life:

Bad Habit	Effect on Work Life

Bad habits affect your job. If you want to keep your job, you will have to work on changing bad habits. If you have developed bad habits since starting work, you must find out why.

Did you pick them up from someone? Or have you decided that these bad habits do not matter on your work site?

You need a SURVIVAL CHECK.
BAD HABITS can be broken.

Good Habits in Your Personal Life

Good habits have a positive effect on most people. Good habits become a part of you and usually make you look good. If you have had your good habits since you were a child, you do not think about them as habits.

You need to stop and think about these good habits. You need to think about what they have done for you and what effect they have had in your personal life.

STOP AND THINK

Look at your sixth-grade list. What good habits are you still carrying around with you? List the habit and how it has affected your personal life:

Good Habit	Effect on Personal Life

(continues)

(continued)

Good Habit	Effect on Personal Life

Good habits have positive effects. They will work to your advantage. You have recognized their positive effects. They will make you look good. They will improve your personal life.

Good Habits in Your Work Life

The good habits that you had in sixth grade can help you on the work site. The comparison will probably surprise you. Good habits in school are good habits at work.

Stop and Think

Take a look at your sixth-grade list. What good habits are you still carrying around with you? List the habit and how it has affected your work life:

Good Habit	Effect on Work Life

Good Habit	Effect on Work Life

Good habits work for you. You now know the effects of good habits and what they have done for you. Good habits that you developed as a child are still working for you in your working adult life.

If you developed these habits after entering a job, then you must have had good reasons. You must have experienced or observed their good effect in the work site.

GOOD HABITS provide a GOOD SURVIVAL GUIDE.

Successful Achievement Using Good Habits

Good habits are a great contributor to success. It is difficult to achieve unless you have developed good habits. Sometimes you forget what really helped you to achieve success.

STOP AND THINK

Everyone has a story to tell. Tell a story about yourself in which you were successful in achieving something. It can be a small or very large achievement. You must be the main person in this achievement.

_____

_____

_____

_____

_____

_____

What habits helped you in this successful achievement?

1. _____ 6. _____

2. _____ 7. _____

3. _____ 8. _____

4. _____ 9. _____

5. _____ 10. _____

Everyone loves a success story. Good habits and success go hand in hand. This is your story using your good habits. Carry good habits right into the work site, and you can have many success stories.

You have a SURVIVAL GUIDE.
You will survive on the job.

Signs of Good and Bad Habits

If you observe a person's house, car, yard, dress, hygiene, or office, you can tell a lot about his or her habits. There are signs that indicate good or bad habits. You need to be aware of these signs about yourself. Start observing signs of habits.

STOP AND THINK

Describe the person who occupies this office:

_____

_____

_____

The Family Circle
■ Cookbook ■
New Taste for New Times

Every Woman's
HEALTH
Caring for Your
Body & Mind

Art Fair

DIPLOMA

DIXIE WRIGHT

LANDSCAPE PLANNING KIT

(continues)

(continued)

List the habits that you think this person has:

1. _____

2. _____

3. _____

4. _____

5. _____

6. _____

7. _____

8. _____

9. _____

10. _____

What makes you think these are habits? _____

_____

If you can recognize signs of habits in other people, then other people can see signs of habits when observing you and your surroundings. Habits show even when you do not expect them to be recognized. Habits definitely show on the work site. Continue your good habits and try eliminating your bad habits.

Be aware of your bad habits. Stop a bad habit as soon as you catch yourself doing it. Do something that will take your mind off the bad habit. Remind yourself how bad habits hurt you. Practice your good habits.

Use your SURVIVAL GUIDE.

CHAPTER 8

This chapter will help you

- Understand what manners are.

- Identify good and bad manners.

- See the effects of manners.

- Learn the magic of good manners.

MANNERS

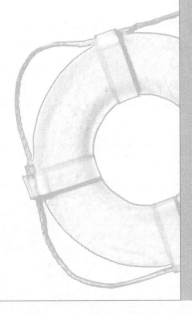

This is your
SURVIVAL ENHANCER.

Manners make a statement about you instantly.

Manners are a form of communication that we rarely think about. But everyone observes your manners.

Something happens when you practice good manners. I call it magic.

This is STUFF YOU NEED TO REALIZE.

What Are Manners?

Manners are a way of acting. Manners are a person's bearing or behavior.

Manners are often overlooked as part of a job. Manners make a statement about you immediately. You may not be aware of your manners. You need to increase your awareness of the way you act (your manners).

EXAMPLE

Examples of good manners are saying "please," "thank you," and "excuse me"; waiting your turn in line; and holding doors for people.

Examples of bad manners are not letting someone finish a sentence; being loud; and not being polite.

People observe the manners of others. People have good and bad manners at different times. You can be conscious or unconscious of your manners.

Look at Good Manners

Most people try to use good manners most of the time.

STOP AND THINK

Name 10 good manners that you think you have:

1. _____

2. _____

3. _____

4. _____

5. _____

6. _____

7. _____

8. _____

9. _____

10. _____

How did you acquire these good manners?_____

_____

_____

Were these manners taught to you as a child? Yes ___ No ___

Were these manners picked up by observing someone else? Yes ___ No ___

Why are these 10 manners important to you? _____

_____

_____

_____

Good manners are either important or not important to you. If they are important to you, it will help your job survival to learn why.

Look at Bad Manners

Everyone will use bad manners sometimes. If good manners are important to you, then bad manners will bother you. They may even disgust you.

Even people who do not put great weight on good manners get disgusted with bad manners. You need to know why.

STOP AND THINK

Name 10 bad manners that disgust you:

1. _____

2. _____

3. _____

4. _____

5. _____

6. _____

7. _____

8. _____

9. _____

10. _____

Do you think people who have these bad manners were taught good manners as a child? Yes ___ No ___

Explain: _____

_____

_____

Do you think people have picked up bad manners by observing someone else? Yes ___ No ___

Why do these manners disgust you? _____

_____

_____

Bad manners can create a negative statement about you. On the work site, manners can have a big effect on your survival.

Manners MATTER!

The Effects of Good Manners

Doing your job well is very important. But it is not the only thing that makes you valuable to your employer.

If you are dealing with customers in a service position, they probably notice your manners first. How you deal with people can make a difference in doing your job.

EXAMPLE

Carmen was a front-desk receptionist for a very active company. She was in charge of 17 phone lines in addition to her duties of greeting people. Carmen was not as fast as she should be on the phone.

Management had spoken to her several times about this problem. Customers were always saying how polite and pleasant she was. Management had concerns but decided to keep Carmen on the job.

Management decided to keep Carmen because the company liked to treat its customers politely. Customers noticed how well they were treated when talking to Carmen.

This was not a small thing for the company. Because most customers talked with Carmen first, she created a good impression of the company. Customers felt special. They received the service and attention they wanted.

STOP AND THINK

Huberto was the manager of an automobile repair shop. It was not a large dealership. It was an independent repair shop. Business continued to grow. Customers

(continues)

(continued)

were willing to wait longer because they liked dealing with Huberto. He made them feel special.

1. Can you explain why the customers liked dealing with Huberto? _____

_____

_____

_____

2. Can you explain why the owner would care whether customers liked Huberto or not? _____

_____

_____

_____

Manners can make the difference in customer satisfaction. They can also make a difference in dealing with coworkers and management. Manners can make a difference in profits.

GOOD MANNERS will ENHANCE your JOB SURVIVAL.

The Effects of Bad Manners

You may not be aware of your annoying manners. You may not consider manners to be important at work. You may consider your actions justified. You may not think of these actions as bad manners.

Your boss is watching more than just your job performance. You are part of a company image. When people find out where you work, they identify you with the company.

If you are doing something that annoys your boss, the boss will consider this when deciding to keep or advance you on the job.

The BOSS is always WATCHING.

EXAMPLE

Elsa was a computer repair technician for a large company. She was very good at what she did. Her ability to assist people over the phone was very good. Elsa was always asking for help from her supervisors. She constantly interrupted them, even when they were speaking with others. Elsa was sent a warning notice.

Why did she get a warning notice? Why did her supervisors care about such a small thing?

This was not a small thing to Elsa's supervisors. Although Elsa was good at what she did, her bad manners affected the department. It is rude to interrupt people when they are talking to others. Elsa interrupted her supervisors as they were helping other people or solving other problems.

Elsa needs to wait her turn. Or, Elsa can make a list of her problems and then set a time to speak with a supervisor.

STOP AND THINK

Charles was a retail clerk in a major department store. He was always on time, never missed work, and his register was seldom wrong.

Many customer complaints were filed against him for being rude. He was very defensive about his rudeness. Charles was dismissed from his job.

(continues)

(continued)

1. Can you explain why Charles was dismissed from his job? _____

_____

_____

_____

2. Can you explain why his supervisor should care about such a small thing? _____

_____

_____

_____

Be aware of your manners in the workplace. Go out of your way to handle every situation with good manners.

You may not consider this important, but other persons might. You may not have the final say.

BAD MANNERS do not ENHANCE your JOB SURVIVAL.

Good Manners Versus Bad Manners

Many people state that manners are not too important—it is more important who a person is.

This may be true. But manners can tell you what you want to know about someone. A good way to realize this is to imagine a first date at a restaurant. In this situation, it would be easy to learn about someone from his or her manners.

GOOD MANNERS make you LOOK GOOD.
BAD MANNERS make you LOOK BAD.

STOP AND THINK

You are on a first dinner date with someone you like. List all the good manners that would impress you:

1. _____

2. _____

3. _____

4. _____

5. _____

6. _____

7. _____

8. _____

9. _____

10. _____

You are on a first dinner date with someone you like. List all the bad manners that would turn you off:

1. _____

2. _____

3. _____

(continues)

(continued)

4. _____

5. _____

6. _____

7. _____

8. _____

9. _____

10. _____

You usually work hard on a first date to impress someone. A first date at a restaurant can tell you a lot about the manners of a person. It can also tell you a lot about your own manners and what you consider good and bad manners.

Feelings About
Good and Bad Manners

You may not realize how you feel when you are around people with bad manners and people with good manners.

STOP AND THINK

1. Does someone in your workplace have exceptionally good manners? Yes ___
   No ___ Describe this person: _____

   _____

   _____

2. How do you feel when you are around this person? _____

_____

_____

3. Does someone in your workplace have exceptionally bad manners? Yes ___

No ___ Describe this person: _____

_____

_____

4. How do you feel when you are around this person? _____

_____

_____

You get busy with your daily routine. Sometimes you do not think how the actions of others make you feel. The daily actions of others can affect you in a positive or negative way.

Manners Send Messages

Manners can sometimes make you or break you when first meeting someone. Manners instantly communicate to a stranger. You must be aware of your behavior (manners).

Be on your BEST BEHAVIOR (good manners).

Manners send messages about you before you have a chance to know someone.

STOP AND THINK

1. What messages can manners send about you in an interview? _____

_____

_____

2. What messages can manners send about you when first meeting coworkers?

_____

_____

3. What messages can manners send about you when first meeting management?

_____

_____

People have not been hired because of bad manners in an interview. Do not make light of manners. Take your manners very seriously. Good manners enhance your position at work.

Manners and Habits Overlap

Many times manners and habits overlap. Using bad manners can become a bad habit. You may be aware that your actions annoy your boss. These actions could cost an advancement or job.

 EXAMPLE

Richard has been working in the warehouse for a book company. He is a good employee and has requested to be transferred to the retail department selling books. He has never been offered this position. His boss has observed that Richard does not cover his mouth when he sneezes or coughs.

What could be the reason he has never been put on the retail floor? The reason is that customers would find Richard's behavior to be rude, offensive, and unhealthy. Richard has bad manners, which have become a bad habit.

STOP AND THINK

1. Nina has been working for the same company for three years. She has put in for advancement to another department several times. Each time she has been passed over. Nina is very impatient when she needs something from her boss. She has expressed this in many ways.

   What could be one reason she is passed over for advancement? _____

   _____

   _____

2. John was hired as a stockperson for a large discount chain store. His job was to stock and assist people to the right department. John was introduced to the general manager. When the general manager extended his hand for a handshake, John slapped his hand and said, "Glad to meet you, brother." John was dismissed from his job.

   What could have been one reason he was dismissed from his job? _____

   _____

   _____

3. Why should manners matter if you are doing your job? Suppose you are representing the company. Explain possible reasons why manners should matter:

   _____

   _____

   _____

If you are doing annoying things—whether they are bad manners or bad habits—these things will have to stop. You need to find out what you are doing that your boss does not like.

Ask your boss. Go directly to him or her. Ask for an appointment to see him or her. Be very polite but ask why you have been passed over for advancement or have lost your job. You need to know because your survival on any job is at risk.

The Magic of Good Manners

One of the best ways to understand yourself and how good manners have worked for you is to think about your personal experiences. By analyzing your experiences, you can see the results.

GOOD MANNERS can WORK MAGIC.

STOP AND THINK

Think of an occasion where you knew you had to be on your best behavior (such as at a wedding reception for a coworker).

1. How did good manners work for you? Tell your story: _____

_____

_____

2. How could good manners work for you in the workplace? _____

_____

_____

If you have experienced a good feeling from showing good manners, then you know how they enhanced your image.

It was LIKE MAGIC.

Could good manners enhance your image in the workplace? Are you showing manners in the workplace that are not your best behavior? You need a manner review.

Review Your Manners

You know what good and bad manners are. You know their effect in the workplace.

You know the MAGIC OF GOOD MANNERS.

You need to know what good and bad manners mean to you personally.

STOP AND THINK

Think about the things you say and do on the work site. Use the "Good" column if the item is good manners. Use the "Bad" column if the item is bad manners. Then, if you do this every day, circle the "E." If you do this occasionally, circle the "O."

Manners	Good		Bad	
Please	E	O	E	O
Thank you	E	O	E	O
Chew gum	E	O	E	O
Hold door for someone	E	O	E	O
Excuse me	E	O	E	O
Belch	E	O	E	O
Use toothpick while working	E	O	E	O

(continues)

(continued)

Manners	Good		Bad	
Use a napkin while eating	E	O	E	O
Blow your nose in front of people	E	O	E	O
Use four-letter words (vulgarity)	E	O	E	O
Pick nose in public	E	O	E	O
Can I help you?	E	O	E	O
Cover mouth when sneezing or coughing	E	O	E	O
Clean fingernails on work site	E	O	E	O
Scratch on work site	E	O	E	O
Open door for someone	E	O	E	O
Talk with your mouth full	E	O	E	O
Pick something up for someone	E	O	E	O
Mr./Mrs./Ms.	E	O	E	O

Look carefully at the number of "O"s you circled. If the items are good manners, do more. If they are bad manners, do less.

Bad manners will hurt you in the workplace. Now that you know what bad manners are, you can start correcting them.

Good manners will work magic for you in the workplace. They will enhance you in everything you do. They will enhance your image and your job survival. Manners make a difference in the workplace.

Manners are YOUR SURVIVAL ENHANCER.

CHAPTER 9

This chapter will help you

- Know your primary job responsibility.

- Know your secondary job responsibility.

- Understand the structure of your workplace.

- See where you fit in this structure.

- Understand the importance of your job.

JOB RESPONSIBILITIES

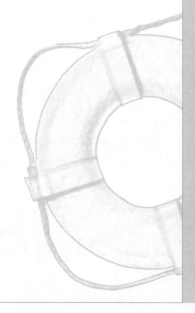

This is your SURVIVAL INSURANCE.

Your primary job responsibility is what you were hired to do.

Other jobs you do on the work site are secondary.

The only person who can change this is your manager or assistant manager.

Your primary responsibility can make a difference in profits.

This is STUFF YOU MUST KNOW.

What Is a Primary Job Responsibility?

Workers often do not know their main job responsibilities. If they do not know their number 1 responsibility, often they will make it equal to other required duties.

This is risky. You must know your job's number 1 responsibility.

STOP AND THINK

Here is a list of common jobs. What do you think would be each job's main responsibility? The first entry is done for you as an example.

Position	Primary Responsibility
Cashier	Running cash register
Chef	
Receptionist	
Data entry clerk	
Mail clerk	
Teacher	
Coach	
Manager	
Assistant manager	
Supervisor	
Auto mechanic	

Position	Primary Responsibility
Driver	
Baby sitter	
Baker	
Hairdresser	
Computer operator	
Janitor	
Salesman	
Courtesy clerk	

You may think that the primary responsibility of a chef is cooking. But at one restaurant, it may be creating recipes. Not all primary and secondary responsibilities are the same for the same jobs. You must know the number 1 reason you were hired.

STOP AND THINK

1. List your job title: _____

2. What is your primary job responsibility? _____

_____

What Is a Secondary Job Responsibility?

Secondary responsibilities are also important. They include duties you are expected to do. Secondary job responsibilities are expected after you have done your number 1 responsibility.

STOP AND THINK

Here is the same list of common jobs. What do you think would be a possible secondary responsibility for each job?

Position	Secondary Responsibility
Cashier	Counting money drawer
Chef	
Receptionist	
Data entry clerk	
Mail clerk	
Teacher	
Coach	
Manager	
Assistant manager	
Supervisor	
Auto mechanic	
Driver	

Position	Secondary Responsibility
Baby sitter	
Baker	
Hairdresser	
Computer operator	
Janitor	
Salesman	
Courtesy clerk	

Many people prefer doing their secondary duties before their number 1 duty. This is very risky. Again, it is important that you know the main job you were hired to do.

STOP AND THINK

1. List your job title: _____

2. What are your secondary job responsibilities? _____

_____

Know your JOB RESPONSIBILITIES.
They are your SURVIVAL INSURANCE.

The Workplace Structure

You must recognize the structure of your workplace to see where your job fits in.

EXAMPLE

Here is where a retail clerk fits into his or her workplace structure: manager, assistant manager, merchandiser, retail clerk, inventory clerk, stocker, and janitor.

The people in these jobs work together on the work site. If one person does not do his or her job, the work site does not function smoothly.

STOP AND THINK

Think about some common workplaces. For each position, list all the jobs that make up its workplace structure.

Position	Jobs in Workplace Structure
Chef	
Hairdresser	
Receptionist	

To survive in the rapidly changing work world, you must start recognizing the structure of the workplace. You must know where you fit in. You must know what your job and job responsibilities mean to the success of the business.

Where You Fit in the Work Structure

You need to know where you fit in the work structure. All coworkers have to work together to make the business successful.

STOP AND THINK

1. Is your primary job important to your workplace structure? Yes ___ No ___

2. Draw a diagram of your workplace structure. Start with the manager. Then include the worker next in line, followed by the worker next in line, and so on:

3. Mark an "X" where you fit into this diagram.

If you know where you fit in the work structure, then you know what you have to do to make the business successful. You have to understand your main and secondary jobs. You have to know what part they play in the total business.

Knowing what YOU HAVE TO DO IS SURVIVAL INSURANCE.

Is Your Primary Job Important to the Business?

Visualize your work site. Visualize the work structure of the work site. Visualize yourself in this work site.

Look at the diagram you just completed.

The manager stands for profit because the manager's main job to look after profit. If there is no profit, the manager will be out of a job.

Look where you have put an "X" on the diagram, which represents your place in the work structure.

STOP AND THINK

1. Is your primary job important to the manager? Yes ___ No ___

   Explain why your job is important: _____

   _____

   _____

2. Is your primary job important to your coworkers? Yes ___ No ___

   Explain why your primary job is important to your coworkers: _____

   _____

   _____

You have identified where you are in the work structure. You have declared whether you think your primary job is important to the business.

If you decide that it is important, then you know it is your responsibility to do your job.

Is Your Secondary Job Important to the Business?

Your secondary job responsibilities are second after your primary job. You must decide if you think they are important to the success of the business.

STOP AND THINK

1. Are your secondary jobs important to the manager? Yes ___ No ___

   Explain why they are important to the manager: _____

   _____

   _____

2. Are your secondary jobs important to your coworkers? Yes ___ No ___

   Explain why they are important to your coworkers: _____

   _____

   _____

3. Do your secondary jobs contribute to the profits of the company? Yes ___ No ___

   How do your secondary jobs contribute to profits? _____

   _____

   _____

You must know your secondary duties. Were they part of your job description? If you say that your secondary responsibilities are important and that they were part of your job description, this means that you must do them.

Be cautious. Don't get caught up in secondary duties. Remember that they are always second to the number 1 reason you were hired.

Protect your SURVIVAL INSURANCE.

Teamwork

You cannot underestimate the importance of teamwork. It is what makes a business run. Good teamwork is what makes a business successful.

Teamwork is very important in the workplace. One person alone cannot do everything, even in a home-based business. Individuals have to "team" with someone to make a profit.

One person alone cannot do everything. But one person alone can spoil everything. It is important that you know how and where you fit on the team.

STOP AND THINK

Think about your "job team" like a sports team. What position would you like to play?

Team	Desired Position
Soccer	
Football	
Baseball	
Basketball	
Hockey	

In thinking about your job as a sports team position, you can see how each position has to work together.

You already know what happens on a sports team when one player does not do the job. This is something you have experienced or observed. Now apply it to your work team.

Good teamwork promotes SURVIVAL INSURANCE.

Your Position on the Job Team

Think about the sports teams. Do you consider certain positions more important than others? Could this position be important without the other players doing their jobs? What about your job team? What about your position? Is it a necessary part of your team?

STOP AND THINK

1. Look at the following teams. Write your desired position and the importance of the position to the team:

Team	Desired Position	Importance of Position
Soccer		
Football		
Baseball		
Basketball		
Hockey		

2. Explain why these positions are important on the sports teams: _____

_____

_____

Are you getting THE BIG PICTURE?

You have favorite positions on a sports team and consider some players more valuable than others. But you know that one person does not make a team.

The same is true in the workplace. Your position or job responsibility is important to the whole team.

A TEAM PLAYER has SURVIVAL INSURANCE.

Team Members Who Distract You

Goals keep you moving. Goals keep you focused. Doing your primary and secondary jobs keeps you working. Watch out for distractions.

Some people in the workplace may distract your team. These people are in every workplace. You must keep focused on your job goal and your main responsibility.

STOP AND THINK

1. Write a short-term goal for work: _____

_____

What do you want this goal to do for you? _____

_____

2. Write a long-term goal at work: _____

_____

What do you want this goal to do for you? _____

_____

You must see your big picture. Do not let distractions put a blot on your big picture. Keep your goals in mind. They will keep you focused on what has to be done to survive on your job. You need all the insurance you can get. Know your primary job responsibility and make sure you do it before other job duties. This will give you great survival insurance.

CHAPTER 10

This chapter will help you

- Understand that every workplace has rules.

- Understand spoken and unspoken rules.

- See the importance of rules in the workplace.

- Know the difference between legal rights and given rights.

HOUSE RULES AND RIGHTS

This is your SURVIVAL ADVANTAGE.

Every business has written rules and regulations.

But it is the spoken and unspoken rules that can cause you trouble.

Every employee has lawful and given rights.

Caution: Know what is a lawful right and what is a given right before you speak.

This is STUFF THAT WILL COST YOU YOUR JOB OR ADVANCEMENT.

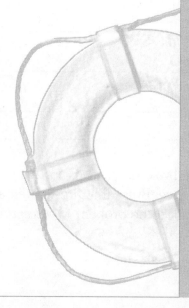

Written Rules

Every business has rules and regulations. Many are safety rules regulated by a state agency. Company rules are written and posted or always available for review in some written form. They are part of employee orientation.

EXAMPLE

Examples of written rules are no smoking, no drugs, and no weapons.

STOP AND THINK

1. List as many rules as you can remember seeing posted in a workplace:

_____

_____

_____

_____

_____

2. Why are these rules posted? _____

_____

3. Who came up with these rules and why? _____

_____

You know the saying "Rules are meant to be broken." No, no, no. They are not meant to be broken, especially in the workplace. Rules that are written and posted are state rules or company rules. They are not to be broken. *No exceptions.* Know these rules or where to review them.

It is to YOUR SURVIVAL ADVANTAGE.

Spoken Rules

Spoken rules are rules that are usually declared by a manager or supervisor. They can differ from business to business. They can differ from department to department.

EXAMPLE

Examples of spoken rules could be no eating on the job and no friends visiting the work site.

STOP AND THINK

1. Name as many spoken rules as you can remember hearing in any workplace. These rules are things a supervisor says you can or cannot do:

   _____

   _____

   _____

   _____

   _____

2. Why is it necessary to speak these rules? _____

   _____

3. Who came up with these rules? _____

   _____

The rules spoken by managers and supervisors are rules they want carried out. It is wise to follow these directions. Not following spoken rules may not cost you the job. But it will cost you your survival advantage.

Unspoken Rules

Unspoken rules are rules you already know to follow in the workplace. These rules involve behaviors, habits, and manners. Breaking these unspoken rules can get you in big trouble.

EXAMPLE

An example is coming to work in a dirty uniform or dirty clothes. Another example is cussing in front of your boss on the work site. You know better than to do these things. The rules do not have to be spoken.

STOP AND THINK

1. Name as many unspoken rules as you can think of. These are rules that no one has to speak to you about. You know not to break these rules without being told:

_____

_____

_____

_____

2. How do you know not to break these rules? _____

_____

_____

3. Who came up with these unspoken rules? _____

_____

_____

The unspoken rules can get you in big trouble. You have to be aware of the consequences when you try to break these rules.

Breaking unspoken rules may not cost you your job immediately. But it may cost you your job if you continue to break them.

Be aware of the UNSPOKEN RULES. You need every SURVIVAL ADVANTAGE you can get.

Things You Would Report

Breaking rules can affect the entire business. Rules and regulations are made to protect and improve the business and workplace.

You may see coworkers break rules. You must determine when and what you are willing to report to your manager. Consider all the consequences. Consider how breaking the rules affects the business, coworkers, and you.

STOP AND THINK

Would you report a coworker to management if you knew the coworker was breaking rules? Evaluate the following situations and put a check mark under "Yes" or "No":

Situation	Yes	No
Coworker has to leave early and asks you to clock out for him.		

(continues)

(continued)

Situation	Yes	No
Coworker is stealing from another coworker.		
Coworker is taking office supplies home.		
Coworker is using business phone for personal calls.		
Coworker is stealing food from breakroom refrigerator.		
Coworker is smoking in no-smoking area.		
Coworker is stealing from cash register.		
Coworker is drinking alcohol on the job.		

The consequences of breaking rules can be major or minor. Ask yourself if you would break the rule, and why or why not. Decide what you think about someone breaking a rule, but do not consider who the person is.

KEEPING RULES can help you ADVANCE ON YOUR JOB.

The Risk of Breaking Rules

Breaking some rules may seem like a small thing. But if allowed to continue, it could cost you your job or interfere in your advancement.

 # EXAMPLE

Carla is a courtesy clerk for a major grocery chain. Carla would take small breaks and eat the samples that were put out for customers. Carla was hungry, and after all, they were free. Carla was told before she started her job that employees could not sample food.

Even though it is not a written rule, Carla could get in trouble for eating samples. It is a spoken rule, and management has reasons for not wanting employees to eat samples.

Although employees may not completely understand why this is a rule, breaking it is a problem. The employer may not want employees chewing on food when talking to customers. The employer is still paying for the samples, even if the store is not charging customers for them. So eating the food is like taking from the employer. Finally, it looks unprofessional for employees to be eating on the job.

Carla could get a warning from her employer about this. Carla could even lose her job if she continued to ignore the rule.

If you are unsure about a rule, ask someone before testing the rule. Coworkers will report the breaking of unwritten rules. You may think no one will notice, but chances are someone will see it and report it.

Do not break unwritten rules. It is risky. It is not in your best interest. Rules are not to be broken in the workplace. It is up to you to foresee the consequences of breaking rules.

Stop and Think

John was a head chef at a large hotel restaurant. The restaurant was struggling to increase profits. John decided to help by refreezing meat if it was not used the day it was thawed.

1. Can John get into trouble for this? Yes ___   No ___   Why would he get into trouble? After all, it is saving money. _____

   _____

   _____

2. Could he lose his job? Yes ___   No ___   Why? _____

   _____

You have to determine if this rule just involves John. Think about the possible consequences of breaking this rule. Is it going to be to John's advantage for job survival?

STOP AND THINK

Dan is a bus driver for the Regional Transportation Company. He has been off for the weekend. He attended a party the night before he was to return to work and woke up with a big hangover. Dan decided to take a stiff drink before going to work.

1. Can Dan get into trouble for this? Yes ____   No ____   Why would he get into trouble? No one will ever know. One drink is nothing. _____

   _____

   _____

2. Could he lose his job over this? Yes ____   No ____   Why? _____

   _____

Again, you have to determine if this rule just involves Dan. Think about the possible consequences of breaking this rule. Is breaking the rule to Dan's advantage for job survival?

Lawful and Given Rights

In the workplace, there are lawful rights and given rights. Many people confuse the two. This can cause serious problems.

- *Lawful rights* are just what they are called. These are rights that you are entitled to in the workplace by law. For example, sexual harassment is unlawful. You have a legal right to have it stopped.

  Make sure you are informed about your legal rights. There is information available on legal rights through the Department of Labor in each state.

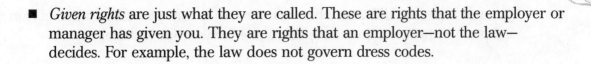

■ *Given rights* are just what they are called. These are rights that the employer or manager has given you. They are rights that an employer—not the law—decides. For example, the law does not govern dress codes.

LAW sets LEGAL rights.
EMPLOYERS set GIVEN rights.

STOP AND THINK

1. List rights you think are yours by law: _____

_____

_____

_____

_____

2. List rights you think are yours because the employer or manager has given them to you: _____

_____

_____

_____

_____

It is your responsibility to know your legal rights. It is not the responsibility of the employer. The employer is responsible for your given rights.

You must know the difference between the two before you make statements in the workplace. Otherwise, this can spell trouble for your job survival.

STOP AND THINK

Cherrie was a clerk working for a large corporation. Cherrie was in the habit of taking several restroom or water fountain breaks. Her supervisor questioned the number of breaks she was taking. Cherrie was angered by the accusation and expressed to coworkers that it was her right to get up as many times as she pleased.

1. Is Cherrie right? Yes ___ No ___

2. Is leaving her job space any business of her supervisor? Yes ___ No ___

3. Is it a given right or lawful right to leave your job space anytime you want?

   _____

4. Can she get in trouble if she continues to leave her job space? Yes ___ No ___

Do not confuse legal and given rights. Educate yourself on legal rights. Inform yourself about given rights in the workplace. Not knowing is a disadvantage for you. Know the difference between legal and given rights before speaking.

STOP AND THINK

Jerome works for a lighting assembly firm. He is scheduled for 40 hours a week. He is often asked to work a little later when the company is behind on orders. He is afraid to say no. It is usually only an additional 45 minutes to an hour, and he needs the job. Jerome does not get overtime pay for this work.

1. Does he have a right to say no to unpaid overtime? Yes ___ No ___

2. Why does he have or not have the right to say no to unpaid overtime? _____

   _____

3. Can he lose his job over this? Yes ＿＿ No ＿＿

4. What are his choices if his employer continues this practice? ＿＿＿＿＿＿＿＿＿＿

＿＿＿＿＿＿＿＿＿＿＿＿＿＿＿＿＿＿＿＿＿＿＿＿＿＿＿＿＿＿＿＿＿

Stop and Think

Maria is working for a telemarketing company. She gets a bonus when she signs more persons than her quota requires. One coworker has received a bonus almost every week. Maria says it is not fair because her supervisor gives her coworker better lists to work from. She says she has the right to the same lists or she is going to report her supervisor to top management.

1. Does she have the right to report her supervisor to top management?

   Yes ＿＿ No ＿＿

2. Could she lose her job if she reports her supervisor? Yes ＿＿ No ＿＿

3. What are her choices if the current situation continues? ＿＿＿＿＿＿＿＿＿＿

＿＿＿＿＿＿＿＿＿＿＿＿＿＿＿＿＿＿＿＿＿＿＿＿＿＿＿＿＿＿＿＿＿

Do not confuse legal and given rights. Knowing and appreciating your legal and given rights can be a great survival advantage.

Legal Rights and Given Rights Review

This review is to test your understanding of the difference between legal and given rights. Hopefully by this time, you have a clear understanding of the difference.

Here is a list of issues related to rights. Put a check mark under "Legal" if you think the issue is governed by law. Put a check mark under "Given" if you think it is something your employer decides.

Issues Related to Rights	Legal	Given
Eating on the job		
Restroom anytime		
Nonsmoking workplace		
Fired for no reason		
Fighting in workplace		
Clocking in late		
Discrimination		
No breaks in eight hours		
Guns		
Phone privileges		
Soft drink can allowed on work site		
Sexual harassment		
Casual dress day		
Flexible time		
Overtime pay		

Law sets legal rights. Given rights are set by the employer. Know the difference. It is your survival advantage.

CHAPTER 11

This chapter will help you

- Understand stress in the workplace.

- Identify good and bad stress.

- Change bad stress.

- Evaluate your job and stress.

- Change overpowering stress to empowering stress.

JOB STRESS

This is your
SURVIVAL SECRET.

You cannot avoid job stress in the workplace.

Good stress pumps you, and bad stress drains you.

Bad stress can be overpowering.

If you have a job that is overpowering your life, something must change.

This is STUFF YOU CANNOT IGNORE.

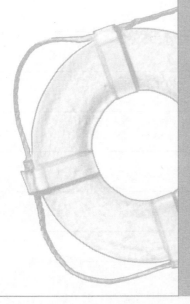

Stress in the Workplace

Stress: A mentally or emotionally disruptive influence.

Stressed: To subject to pressure or strain.

Stress is different things to different people in the workplace. What is stressful for me may not be stressful for you. What is stressful for you may not be stressful for me.

EXAMPLE

Job stress is unavoidable in the workplace. Examples include the following:

- The pressure of a deadline.

- Many customers waiting for service.

- Someone hovering over you to finish your work.

- Having to meet a quota.

STOP AND THINK

Write your definition of stress in the workplace. Give specific examples of stress.

1. My definition of stress in the workplace is _____

   _____

   _____

2. This was stressful for me: _____

   _____

3. This was stressful for me: _____

   _____

4. This was stressful for me: _____

_____

Bad stress can affect you in many ways, including the following:

- Slow you down.

- Interfere with your thought process.

- Harm your health.

- Affect your appetite.

- Definitely affect your work life.

You need to identify what is stressful for you. You need to learn how to cope with it.

This is YOUR WORK SECRET.

Good and Bad Stress

You have identified bad stress. You know how it can affect your daily personal life and your daily working life. You know bad stress can drain you. But did you know that good stress can motivate you and keep you moving?

GOOD STRESS can MOTIVATE.
BAD STRESS can DRAIN.

STOP AND THINK

Look at the following list. Write an "M" if this type of stress can motivate you. Write a "D" if this type of stress can drain you.

(continues)

(continued)

____ Deadlines	____ Conflicts
____ Someone watching you	____ Holiday preparations
____ Following specific instructions	____ Ill health
____ More than one assignment at same time	____ Overtime
____ Long hours	____ Crowded conditions
____ Bad weather	____ Too many bosses
____ Rainy driving conditions	____ Money matters
____ Children	____ Pressure at work
____ Spouse	____ Competition
____ Special events	____ Jealousy
____ Arguments	____ Lack of time

All stress is not bad. All stress is not harmful to your health. All stress is not harmful to you in the workplace.

You need to look at your list above, and recognize what is bad and what is good stress in your life.

Overpowering Stress

You must be concerned about the bad stress that is draining you. Stress that is draining you can cause problems. To cope with this stress, you must find out where the stress is coming from and what is the cause.

 STOP AND THINK

How many "D"s do you have listed above? _____

These are overpowering stress makers. They may be overtaking your working and personal life.

Write the items that you marked as "D"s:

_____   _____

_____   _____

_____   _____

_____   _____

_____   _____

_____   _____

Next to each item above, write the number of the item from below causing the stress. There may be more than one number:

1. Boss   4. Lack of skills   7. Fatigue

2. Coworkers   5. Bad time management   8. Job pressure

3. Personal problems   6. Health problems   9. All of these

You cannot do a good job if stress is overpowering your life. It is draining you. You must identify and work on the cause of your stress.

This is your SURVIVAL SECRET.

Change Your Bad Stress

Once you have identified the cause or causes of your overpowering stress, you can start to work on changes. If changes can be made, do so before you risk your job security. If it is something you cannot change, then you have to make a decision about your job.

You will not be able to endure
IF YOUR JOB IS OVERPOWERING.

STOP AND THINK

1. What is causing you the most stress on the job? _____

   Explain: _____

   _____

2. What can you do to change the effect of this stress? _____

   _____

   _____

If the stress is overwhelming and cannot be changed, you will have to change jobs. Your job should improve your life, not consume it.

Bad, overpowering stress cannot continue in your life. The consequences are too costly. The price is too high to pay. You must work to change this overpowering stress. Try to change as much as you can.

This is your SURVIVAL SECRET.

Is This the Job for You?

You have identified the bad, overpowering stress and the causes. Is your job the major factor in this stress? If it is, you must think about the importance of this particular job.

STOP AND THINK

Many people have endured jobs that were very stressful to reach their long-term goal.

Think about your long-term goal. Visualize yourself reaching your long-term goal. Then circle "Yes" or "No" to the following questions:

Does this job bring you closer to your goal?	Yes	No
Does this job help you moneywise?	Yes	No
Does this job's hours work with your personal life?	Yes	No
Does this job allow you personal time?	Yes	No
Does this job answer your needs right now?	Yes	No
Does this job prepare you for future plans?	Yes	No
Is this job in a good location for you?	Yes	No
Is this job necessary for your goal?	Yes	No
Is this job worth making changes for?	Yes	No

If most answers are "Yes," start making changes. If most answers are "No," change jobs.

You will not remain on a job that is creating bad stress and overpowering your life—unless you are determined to keep the job and work on the stress.

This is your decision and only your decision to make. How important is this job to you and your goals?

Remember, there are many jobs but only one of you. This is your decision. It is your survival secret.

Things You Have to Do This Week

Consider your priority list and your goals when making your decision. All jobs have some bad stress. Change is not easy. If your job is worth keeping, it is worth changing the bad stress.

STOP AND THINK

Remember your priorities from Chapter 2. Does this job satisfy most of your priorities? Yes ___ No ___ If it does, you must work to eliminate the bad stress. Start by writing the things you have to or want to do this week. Start with first things first:

1. _____   6. _____

2. _____   7. _____

3. _____   8. _____

4. _____   9. _____

5. _____   10. _____

Do not go to the second thing until you have done the first. Do not go to the third thing until you have done the second, and so on. This will organize you and help your stress level.

Bad stress has to go if it is overpowering your life. Job survival is at risk. Changes have to take place. Finishing work-related things you have to do is a good start.

This is a SURVIVAL SECRET.

Your Wish List to Reduce Stress

People who experience a lot of bad stress will often make excuses to themselves and others about their stress level. It is like this: "I am stressed out because…."

Many times this involves excuses about money or something that gives them reason for the stress that other people can accept.

STOP AND THINK

Many times people rationalize that they would have less stress if they had more money.

1. Do you think more money could reduce your stress level? Yes ___   No ___
   Why do you think that? Explain: _____

   _____

   _____

2. Do you know people who have little money yet do not seem overstressed?
   Yes ___   No ___   Why do you think this is? Explain: _____

   _____

   _____

3. Can you reduce your stress through ways that do not cost money?
   Yes ___   No ___   Explain:_____

   _____

   _____

4. Make a wish list that could help reduce your stress:_____

   _____

   _____

   _____

Being honest about your bad stress is hard to do. But being honest with yourself should not be hard to do. Find the cause. Work on the cause. Work on the change.

This can be your SURVIVAL SECRET.

Turn Overpowering Stress to Empowering Stress

Good stress is good for you, and you have already identified it. You do, however, need to recognize what good stress can do for you in your working life and how you have made it work for you.

When you start to balance your work life with your personal life, your life starts to be enriched. Your job changes from overpowering to empowering. This is good stress.

Empowerment changes your life. It gives you more control. It helps you to be motivated and to work harder. It creates security on your job and less bad stress.

Bad stress turns to good stress because YOU HAVE CONTROL.

STOP AND THINK

1. Can you think of a time that you were empowered or motivated to take on a task that you knew would be stressful? Yes ___ No ___ Explain: _____

   _____

   _____

2. Did you have control? Yes ___ No ___

3. Were you determined to succeed? Yes ___ No ___

4. Did you succeed? Yes ___ No ___

5. Was it good stress or bad stress? _____

6. How did the empowerment feel? _____

_____

_____

Changing bad stress to good stress can be done. Changing overpowering stress to empowering stress can be done. There is nothing you cannot improve if it is important to you.

Your job is your means of making money, but it is also your lifetime work. Stress plays a big part in your job survival.

Work on stress: THIS IS YOUR SURVIVAL SECRET.

Your Understanding of Stress

The best test of your understanding of good and bad stress is knowing what you would pass on to children or young adults.

Adults are not the only people who feel stress. Children failing in school are very stressed. Young adults falling behind in schoolwork are stressed.

STOP AND THINK

1. If you were counseling a sixth-grade student who is failing in school, what methods would you use to motivate the student to change bad stress to good stress? _____

_____

(continues)

(continued)

2. What changes would you recommend? _____

_____

_____

3. Do you think it is possible to change bad stress into good stress? Yes ___   No ___

Explain: _____

_____

_____

What we pass on to children is what we think is important to understand. Understanding the effects of good and bad stress and how to cope with this stress is valuable information.

Working on changes is a part of life and everyday living. Working on changes in the workplace is a part of work life. Stress can change from bad to good.

How you do this is your SURVIVAL SECRET.